Saying It Out Loud

A YOUNG WIDOW'S TRIUMPH OVER TRAGEDY

Amy King *with* JON LAND

A POST HILL PRESS BOOK
ISBN: 979-8-89565-437-8
ISBN (eBook): 979-8-89565-438-5

Saying It Out Loud:
A Young Widow's Triumph Over Tragedy

Cover design by Cody Corcoran
Cover photo by Stephanie Leigh Photography and Design

This is a work of nonfiction. All people, locations, events, and situations are portrayed to the best of the author's memory.

This book, as well as any other Post Hill Press publications, may be purchased in bulk quantities at a special discounted rate. Contact orders@posthillpress.com for more information.

Post Hill Press
New York • Nashville
posthillpress.com
Published in the United States of America
1 2 3 4 5 6 7 8 9 10

My dearest Adalyn, this book is for you.
My wish is that you read it and, one day,
your dada becomes alive to you.
Here's the story of your parents.
I love you to the moon and back.

To Andy, I love you forever. May our story never be
forgotten and our love live forever in our daughter's heart.
I will carry you forward with us. Until we meet again.

What we once enjoyed and deeply loved we can never lose,
for all that we love deeply becomes a part of us.

—Helen Keller

CONTENTS

PART THREE: THE TREES

PREFACE

Finding the Joy

We have two lives, and the second begins
when we realize we only have one.
—Confucius

That's become one of my all-time favorite quotes, in large part because I've found myself living it for the past year.

How often do we hear or use the phrase "life is short"? So often, I'd venture to say, that it's become a cliché. But it stops being that when suffering a tragedy makes you realize how true those words are.

At the age of twenty-seven, I lost my husband Andy in an Army Reserve training accident just short of his twenty-eighth birthday. His death left me to raise our then seventeen-month-old daughter Adalyn alone. That's when I began my second life, and I wrote this book to let others know that while you can still find the joy in life, you have to work harder at it.

As a society, we often find ourselves mired in a victim's mentality. This thing or that thing happened, and we tend to let those things define us and bring us down. But we're really here for only a short period of time, and every minute we waste sweating the small stuff is a minute we're not looking for the joy in life.

This book covers the year that followed Andy's death, and to a great extent, it feels like I lost that year not only to grief but to getting used to my second life. And what has helped lift me from the doldrums of that darkness is the realization that grief and joy can exist together, that they are not mutually exclusive. Everyone has darkness in their lives, whether it involves finances, relationship issues, career problems, health, your children—pretty much anything. That darkness tends to dominate us to the point where it can block the light like a total eclipse of the sun.

Don't let it.

The problem we're facing in the present always seems like the worst thing possible, until something worse happens. I've learned the best way to deal with that is to live in the moment. Andy and I had our struggles and problems, and I wish we would have been able to find the joy more. Hindsight is everything. We can't go back, but we can try to do better. The challenge I face now is finding it alone and doing everything I can to help Addie find hers too.

My dad died five years before the accident that claimed Andy. It hit me really hard, but it didn't change my life the way Andy's death did. I make my grocery lists in the Notes app on my iPhone, so every time I open it up to find my list, I find two eulogies there, the one I wrote for my dad and the other for Andy. Nothing helps keep my perspective on things steadier than scrolling past the milk, bread, and eggs listings to be confronted by that reality, the experience of those two funerals dwarfing experiences like a car cutting me off, a delivery showing up late, or a contractor falling behind on a job.

I saw this social media post not too long ago that posed the questions, *If you knew you weren't going to make it home for dinner tonight, what would you do??How would you spend your day?* Who would warrant a phone call? Who would you visit in person? It's so easy and natural to get worked up over the little things, until you've experienced something big and bad.

I've learned not only to avoid wasting time on trivial things but also to no longer bother with negative people, seeking out and creating the positive instead, relying on the community Andy and I had already erected around us. If I didn't know it already, I learned the true value of small-town life in the wake of his passing. That's not something you think about a lot, until it's all you're left with. Andy's gone, but he's still very much a part of me, living in every decision I make. I know how he thought to the point where I know how he'd react to virtually anything, meaning we're still making many decisions together. When it comes especially to Addie, maybe we always will.

I experienced the Five Stages of Grief to some extent because everyone in my position does. But no two people experience them the same way, even though we're part of a club nobody wants to join. The first stage, Denial, struck me in the sense that for a couple of months it felt like Andy was away at Army training and would be coming home, walking through the door at any moment. Almost like my brain was telling me that to provide some peace for my tortured psyche.

It's natural when you lose someone in an accident that was preventable to experience the second stage, Anger. Sure, there were times I was really angry at the Humvee driver and the Army, even Andy at times. But more of my anger was turned toward the loss in general. I had been taking Adalyn to the Little Gym for a class in toddler gymnastics in the year she was born, and I was a stay-at-home mom. We stopped going when she was a year old, and I decided to return after Andy's passing so that I could get good one-on-one time with our daughter, away from the grief and heaviness of our schedule without Andy in it anymore. All the same moms were there. Some were expecting their second child, others their third, and some had new babies with them, while I felt frozen in time. None of these young women knew me that well, and none of them had ever met Andy.

"Oh, hey, Amy, where have you been? We missed you," came the typical greeting.

The class was thirty minutes from our hometown of Woodstock, Virginia, and none of them had probably heard about Andy. So here I was looking at the women who were pregnant or already had multiple kids, and it made me angry, because while their families were getting bigger, mine had gotten smaller.

I ended up canceling my membership that day. It was one of those moments that you think is going to help you but ends up spiraling you back into a time machine to a point in your life that doesn't exist anymore. There are many places I can't return to, because it feels like I am going back in time, visiting my old life, but someone is missing and they aren't going to be there. It is the feeling of being homesick, and there is no home to make that feeling go away. There is no relief that exists. You just have to feel it and let yourself go right through it.

Anger also appeared with family when they tried so hard to help me but ended up making me feel worse. Andy and I had our routines, our system to maintain normalcy, especially with Addie. I got so angry at having to explain every little thing to everyone who just wanted so badly to help. Like Adalyn likes her banana whole, not cut up. We only wash her hair on Fridays. Her sound machine is supposed to be set at 24 percent with the dryer sound and 8 percent with the red light. So many little things that go unspoken in your routine with your partner, and when they are gone it becomes so obvious how deeply that person was a piece of you.

Bargaining is the third stage of grief, and I've come to equate that with rationalization. I tell myself that the accident spared Andy an even worse fate, that if he'd survived it, he was going to die of cancer instead after a painful, years-long struggle. I guess that equates to trying to believe this all happened for a reason in order to lend some purpose to it. *This prevented him from suffering something worse* is how I bargain it in my mind.

Depression is something else that occurs naturally in the grieving process, and I found myself battling it initially by going into task mode. Two days after the funeral, I brought copies of the death certificate to places like the bank and the town hall to have Andy's name taken off the rolls. Keeping busy was a way of dissociating, and that worked until winter set in. I crashed when the days grew short. I'd take Addie to day care and go right back to bed because insomnia was keeping me up at night, telling myself it was okay to spend a chunk of the day in bed because I was sick and had the medications to prove it.

I began to feel better with the coming of spring, maybe because the meds started to kick in, the weather turned, and my denial was turning into my reality. Who knows. Who knows if we ever accept something like this in our brain. I've been told by numerous therapists that Andy's death is the hardest type to accept and that it is actually impossible for your brain to ever fully realize you will never see this person again, because it was traumatic, I didn't see the accident, I didn't see the body, and it was sudden. Andy died in one second. One of his last texts read `I'm in a loud military vehicle, I'll call you in 15 minutes.` He left on a Thursday and returned the following Sunday in a body bag, and days later his duffel bags and belongings that I watched him pack on Wednesday night were returned to me by a different man in uniform.

I don't believe closure or acceptance exists in a situation like this. I think it just becomes a part of you and who you are becoming. Acceptance is more about being at peace with your situation. And I've gotten around to believing that we're all going to the same place; Andy just got there ahead of me. For me, acceptance is a matter of accepting the new relationship I have with him. When someone you love dies, your relationship doesn't end when you put them in a box.

I want to celebrate and keep him alive in memory and spirit, while continuing to build the new relationship I have with him. Death is not the end people think it is, at least it doesn't have to be. When we find a feather, I tell Addie it's from her dad. When thunder roars, I tell her that's her dad laughing. On Andy's first birthday after the accident, we blew out one candle together.

Here's what I posted on Facebook that day:

> This one hurts. Forever twenty-seven. Happy First Heavenly Birthday to my soulmate. Today, I am not strong and I do not have the words. You should be here. But looking at these photos, I would do this all over again, even knowing the outcome. I love you.

Along with that, I posted a number of still shots and videos of Andy and me together, with the dogs, Andy holding Adalyn, Andy being Andy. Viewing the montage now, it looks like the fast-motion trailer for a movie in which Andy was the star. In one shot, he's holding Addie at the top of a slide, ready to let her go so she can make the short trip down without him. There's something eerie about that now, and I'm glad it's a picture instead of a video, because that way I never have to see Andy giving her that little push and letting her go, not realizing he was about to do so forever.

On Andy's next birthday, we're going to blow out two candles.

I organized a memorial 5K race for Andy because it will bring everyone together to do something he loved, and it will make us think of him in a good way. I also started a memorial scholarship fund that will support agriculture students, another passion of Andy's. You can make whatever you want out of life, but you can also make more out of death. It's all about living in the moment and finding the joy, no matter how elusive it might be.

At Andy's funeral, we played a song by Tim McGraw called "Standing Room Only" that seems to pop up everywhere now on the radio when I'm driving. The song feels like it was written about Andy, both figuratively and literally.

The song talks about shining a guiding light. And that's why I wrote this book, that's why I'm saying it all out loud. I hope whatever you are going through in your life, this book encourages you to do something good with it, to shine a light.

PROLOGUE

The Call

An unknown number ran across my phone.

"Ma'am, I'm following behind an ambulance that has your husband in the back."

I could hear the shakiness in the voice of Andy's commanding officer, who at the time I didn't know, and I knew from the second he said *ma'am* nothing would ever be the same again. If you have received a drop-to-your-knees phone call like that, you know the feeling. You've memorized the feeling, and your body will never forget it. At twenty-seven, this would be the second time I knew that feeling.

"There has been an accident," the voice continued, "and I need you to drive to Richmond VCU Trauma Center."

I knew in that moment that my husband was dead, and I prayed to God I would survive it. It was a gut feeling like none I experienced before.

The first time I received a call like that was when I was twenty-two. It was around 5:45 in the morning, and I was on vacation with Andy's family. My phone rang and rang. I lay in bed wide awake ignoring the ring, filled with an awful trepidation I can neither describe nor explain.

Dad is dead, I told myself. *I want just one more moment of him not being dead.*

A minute later, Andy's phone started ringing. Unlike me, he stirred and answered the call. "Hello."

It was my sister asking for me.

"Amy, it's about Dad," she said, after Andy handed me the phone, her voice low and cracking.

"Is it bad, or really bad this time?" I asked her.

"It's really bad."

Neither one of us wanted to say it out loud.

I was in my house alone on a beautiful, sunny, and warm November afternoon in central Virginia when I received the call around 2:20 p.m. from Andy's commanding officer in the Army Reserve. I asked him to text me what he had just said, because my ears were ringing and the walls felt like they were caving in on me. He must have said Richmond VCU (Virginia Commonwealth University) Trauma Center three times, and I still could not remember. We hung up and his text came in. Immediately I got on our laptop to look at Andy's Find My iPhone app. I watched his phone and Apple Watch traveling along I-95 headed into Richmond. I called my mom. My hands were shaking so badly I could barely type the numbers correctly.

No answer.

I called my sister.

No answer.

I called my friend asking her to pick up Adalyn from day care. She was out of town. I finally reached someone, my sister's husband, and told him I needed someone to drive me to Richmond. He started calling everyone.

Finally, my mom called back. "Pack a bag," she said.

"No," I told her, offering no further explanation.

Everyone was under the impression I should pack for weeks, that Andy would probably be having surgeries, and I needed to be prepared to stay there through the duration of that arduous process. But I was already convinced otherwise.

I called my sister-in-law. "Caylee, I think he's dead."

Her husband Adam, Andy's older brother, kept saying, "This is Andy we are talking about. He's so strong and healthy. He's going to be fine."

"No, I don't think so, Adam. Not this time."

I can't explain why I was so certain. Generally, I'm the ultimate optimist, doing my best to see the world the way my seventeen-month-old daughter Addie did. But there was no rainbow in the sky that day or any unicorns anywhere to be seen.

My mom and sister were already headed my way, thirty minutes out. For that half hour, I paced my house. I went from sitting in my car to walking around the house, then back to the car. I kept checking Andy's location on our computer and saw he was at the hospital. I called the day care and gave permission for essentially anyone to pick Addie up because I had no idea who it would be. I found myself in our closet, hugging Andy's clothes certain he would never wear them again. I paced our hallways, studying the family photos hanging on a wall that would have no new ones to offer. I could feel him, and I remember looking at his photo and saying to myself, "I know you are dead. Please God, help me."

I knew Andy was no longer Earth-side. My phone was blowing up, and I was amazed at how quickly people had learned what was happening. Bad news travels faster than good, which can be a positive thing when you need those closest to you to rally to your side. But their reassurances felt hollow and their urgings to hold fast to hope empty.

Finally, an unknown number flashed across the screen. "Ms. King, I am a social services worker at VCU Trauma Center. I wanted to check in and see if you are on the way and how long until you would be here."

I told her I hadn't left yet, that I was alone and needed to arrange childcare and someone to drive me.

"Is Andy…is my husband alive?" I managed to ask, forcing each word from my mouth.

I already knew the answer. If Andy were alive, this would be a surgeon on the line, not a social services worker.

"I'm not authorized to have that information," she said.

"Please, I'm two hours away, and I'm not leaving until someone tells me whether my husband is alive. I can't sit through a drive not knowing"

"I'll see what I can do," she promised.

Five long minutes after I hung up, I got a call from the hospital. "Ms. King, I was the surgeon in the ER when your husband was brought in. He was involved in a serious accident. When paramedics arrived on the scene, they could immediately see that he had suffered a traumatic brain injury."

In that very moment my mom and sister walked through the door.

"Soldiers in his convoy," the surgeon continued, "immediately started working on him, and paramedics were on scene within sixty seconds. You could not have asked for a faster response time. Mrs. King, we did everything we could, but he did not make it."

There it was. The news I had been expecting almost since Andy's commanding officer had addressed me as "ma'am" was finally unleashed into the universe. As I listened to the surgeon explain what I already knew, my mom was motioning for me to hurry and get in the car. I remember shaking my head at her and telling her we weren't going, because there was no need. I don't even remember if I was crying at that moment, what I was feeling. To call it shock would be an understatement.

An hour before, Andy and I were texting about his unit in the Army Reserve almost reaching their destination. Now, he was gone. No more texts. No more words to be spoken. Nothing else to be said. No more chances. No final goodbyes.

The chaplain at the hospital called me shortly after the surgeon.

"Mrs. King, I want you to know that when we realized Andy's body could not take anymore, the entire ER staff and myself held Andy and prayed over him as he passed."

It's an image I can't get out of my head. I'm grateful they did that but heartbroken that I couldn't.

I remember walking out to my porch and sitting down. I looked up, and a contingent of my closest friends were walking up the driveway. Seconds later, my porch was full. My pastor, my friends, my family—my people, the ones I cared about the most, were with me. You can't really console someone in the raw aftermath of such an unspeakable tragedy, but you can comfort them, if not with your words, then with your mere presence.

I kept repeating, "I can't believe this," like the most broken record of all time.

My sister kept telling me to keep saying it, because that's what I was thinking and feeling. So, *I can't believe this* kept spilling out of my mouth. I probably said it a hundred times, maybe a thousand.

I could say I felt numb, but it was more than that. Almost like the world had spun off its axis and everything was out of kilter. When people spoke, sometimes it sounded like a foreign language. When they touched me, it felt like I'd gotten an electric shock from a poorly grounded socket. When they hugged me, I felt Andy's arms wrapped around me.

There is no cushion for the shock of sudden tragedy, no strength to fall back on or comfort to be had. You wake up from a bad dream feeling vast relief, but I wouldn't be waking up from this. Instead, every time I did, a new reality would greet me.

Over the next few weeks, I heard my friends question God.

I didn't do that.

They asked my pastor for answers.

I knew there were none coming.

"Are you mad at God?" they would ask me.

I wasn't sure what I was mad at then, but I knew it wasn't God. I needed Him to be by my side. I needed to feel Him there.

And I have. Ever since.

My daughter Adalyn is two and a half years old now. Every night before bed she kisses a picture of her and her dada together hanging on the wall. The same photo I looked at that November day and begged for God to help me. It makes her feel close to him, like he's still there. Sometimes I feel him too, but he isn't there, and I can't hug him through the glass of a picture frame the way my toddler can.

The second hardest moment of my life was seeing Adalyn walk through the door that evening. I remember around four-thirty I asked my sister to go and pick her up from day care.

"Are you sure?" people asked me. "She can stay until 6 if you need more time."

I wanted her home. The last piece of Andy. I needed to hug her so badly. I will never forget her walking into the house from day care with a bunch of tear-filled faces on her porch and living room, me in the center of it. She was all smiles. No idea in the world that she would never see her dada again.

I want to tell you about what I've been through. I want to be for you what so many were for me, the ones who came striding up the walk to help me find the light in my darkest moments. I want to share my journey as a road map to help you through whatever you have suffered.

By saying it out loud.

PART ONE

THE ELEPHANT IN THE ROOM

AMY KING

Elephant in the Room.
Everyone wants me to talk about it,
The elephant in the room.
I don't want them to know about it,
It's all just way too soon.
How does the world keep spinning around? It
Shouldn't, there's no moon.
How can they ask me to talk about it,
The elephant in the room?
Everyone wants me to talk about it,
The elephant in the room.
I'm scared that if I start, I'll cry out
My emotions will consume.
I know the world must keep turning around
but I'm not ready to resume.
I know I'll have to talk about it
The elephant in the room.
Well I guess it's time to talk about it,
The elephant in the room.
Everyone can see I'm sad about it
But I'm giving myself room.
The world will still keep spinning on and
Past this sadness, I'll resume.
I just have to talk about it,
The elephant in the room.
There we go, I talked about it.
The elephant in the room.
I'm breathing and the weight around it
I'm ready to assume.
The world turns to a better dawn
But it still feels like way too soon.

But now that I have talked about it,
There's no elephant in the room.

Alex King
(reprinted with permission)

CHAPTER 1

Glow Sticks

Our daughter Addie's first word wasn't *mama* or *dada*.

It was *puppy*.

We have two English springer spaniels and a border collie mix we picked up the first year after I graduated from Virginia Tech one year early and Andy still had a year to go. He wanted to get me a dog for Christmas, but the litter wasn't due until the spring. So, Andy had the breeder write a letter at Christmastime attesting to the fact that there was a puppy coming and we'd have the pick of the litter.

When we got the call a few months later, off we went to select the best female the litter had to offer. We scrutinized all the girl puppies, trying to make our decision, and the whole time this male kept hanging around us, even though we were ignoring him. All of a sudden, I looked down and realized he was still right there.

"You know," I said to Andy, "I think he likes us."

And that's how we ended up with our first English springer we named Duke. Our second one, another male named Ryder, was born the same day my dad passed away. It turned out Andy had to leave after the funeral for six months of training in the Army Reserve, giving me an excuse to get Ryder. I wanted something to keep me distracted from grief and it felt meant to be, given the day he was born.

Our third dog, the border collie mix, turned out to be a COVID puppy. Andy had found a litter. He loved animals so much, he would have brought the whole brood home if he could.

"Absolutely not," I told him. "Two's enough. More than enough."

Then about a month later he walked through the door with a big bouquet of flowers in one hand and a dog from the litter he'd told me about in the other. We named her Bailey.

"She's gonna be my work dog here," Andy assured me. "You won't even see her, because she'll be in the truck with me every day. You won't even know she's there."

True to his word, he began packing Bailey into the truck with him every morning, but a problem surfaced: She got carsick and has stayed home with me ever since. Bailey was Addie's favorite of the three, and her name was actually the second word my daughter spoke. Not *mama* and *dada*, but *puppy* and *Bailey*.

Every day, as soon as Andy got home, Addie would run up to him and say, "Puppy, puppy!"

We'd try to get her to say mama or dada, but she wasn't having it, until she finally uttered *mama* and, in short order after that, *dada* around a month before Andy passed. One of the oddities of our situation is that she's now graduated to *mommy* with me but when she talks about Andy, it's still always *dada*. She'll go up to his flag, or his hat, or any of his things and say, "That's Dada's hat!" or "Dada's flag!" Never *daddy*. The word "dada" is frozen in time here. And we have four family portraits hanging in the hall on the way to her room. She points at herself and says, "Baby

Addie!" not "Addie." A constant reminder for me that Andy isn't getting to see her grow up. In every photo and video from when he was alive, she is a baby.

Addie's a horrible sleeper, meaning we had to keep to a very specific bedtime routine, part of which was a bath. After Andy passed, I felt it really important to stick to that routine. Even though I've had so much help from relatives and friends ever since The Call, I try to keep bedtime to just us, only me putting her down almost every night. The bath and bedtime routine was very sacred to Andy and me. Andy worked long hours, but he almost always made it home for our little routine every night.

I will never forget the first routine without him the night following The Call. Twenty-four hours prior, he was sitting right there with me on the tile floor leaning over the bathtub to play with Addie. And now it was just me. Part of her routine after the bath is saying "night, night" to the four photos in the hallway. Her favorite portrait is the one of her and Andy together, and one night, out of nowhere, she leaned forward as I was holding her and kissed him through the glass. Since then, kissing the photo has become a part of our nightly ritual. It's the last thing she does before she goes to sleep.

Adults deal with loss their way and children, of course, in an entirely different manner, and that can lead to moments that are both mesmerizing and emotionally wrenching at the same time. The day I got The Call, friends and family were coming in and out of my house all day and night. Some of Andy's very good friends came over late that evening. One of them walked in wearing a hat like Andy always wore. They worked for the same company, Helena, so the hat had the same logo. Addie is normally very shy—she has stranger danger—but she kept reaching for Andy's friend, over and over.

"She wants you to pick her up," his father told him.

The living room full of people grew quiet as everyone realized what Adalyn was thinking.

Andy's other older brother Alex, meanwhile, looks just like him. From a distance, they could be twins. We FaceTimed everyone on Andy's birthday, and Addie was telling everyone all day, "It's Dada's birthday! It's Dada's birthday!" When we FaceTimed with Alex, he was wearing a hat like Andy did, which made the resemblance even stronger.

"Dada! Dada!" Addie kept saying.

Alex remained silent, no idea what to say. She really thought he was Andy, so what were we supposed to do?

I lost it, the first time since Andy passed that I had to leave the room and go out onto the front porch to cry my eyes out and scream. And moments like that have happened many times since, especially with Andy's brothers, Alex and Adam. In those initial months after The Call, she referred to both of them as "dada" when she saw their photos. Although it was hard for me, I am grateful for the resemblance because it made Addie create a very strong bond with both of them. They look and feel familiar to her. She grew comfortable with them faster than anyone because of that, and I am grateful to them becoming father-like figures for her.

Bringing Bailey home the way he did was so like Andy! His thinking was always to the effect of *Why would we not do this?* It also defined the great success he experienced working for a company called Helena Agri-Enterprises, selling agricultural products like seed, fertilizer, pesticide, and herbicide to local farmers. He had more than four hundred customers covering a large swath of land from all over Virginia to Maryland and West Virginia. His driven approach was about choosing to ask for forgiveness instead of permission. With Andy, it was never *How are we gonna do this?* or *Why should we do this?* It was always *We're going to do this!*

At his funeral, the farmers he serviced got together and brought a huge bushel of corn from all their farms with them as a token of how much they loved working with him, as a person as much as a sales rep. Our friend Chad, who organized it, got up to speak as he brought the bushel onto the stage and said, "I was worried that Andy would be surrounded by too many flowers at his funeral and not enough corn." Corn was the primary crop he serviced, so when I went to pick out his headstone I had a special request.

"Can you put a corn plant on his headstone?"

The headstone maker wasn't too enthused about the prospect. "We've never done that before," he said.

But he was basically the only game in town for the whole Shenandoah Valley.

"I'll see what I can do," he promised.

Then he came back with an alternative.

"Can we do wheat instead? Because we do a lot of wheat, thanks to its importance in Christianity."

I thought that sounded okay. Andy had worked with wheat too, not just corn. If wheat's easier, I figured, let's go with that. But when we spoke, that's not what came out of my mouth.

"No," I told him, "it's got to be corn."

"Okay," he relented. "I'll send you a sketch of what we can do."

And, with that, an ear of corn ended up engraved on Andy's headstone, maybe the first one anywhere to be so graced.

He was always the fun parent, while I was the control freak. Addie didn't crawl until she was something like ten months old, and we'd later learn she started walking at day care weeks before walking for us. Addie never liked to do anything until she mastered it, or, in this case, she didn't want us to see her do it until she had the toddler walk down pat. I think she wanted to keep being held and snuggled for as long as possible.

The first time we actually witnessed her walking was captured in one of the last videos featuring Andy and Adalyn together. He wanted her to play basketball so badly—at least the toddler version, which consisted of a hoop just a little taller than she was and a little soft basketball. I remember when we got the basketball hoop. It was one of our last outings together. We went to Target and were walking all the aisles for fun. Andy came across this basketball hoop that he insisted on purchasing for our barely walking toddler. He would sit there all day and put her up to the hoop, showing her how to put the little ball through the net. Then he'd set her down and encourage her to walk over and bring the ball back to do it again. Finally, after scoring a basket, she pushed herself up and made it over to the ball. She dropped down to pick it up, then brought it back to him. I don't know whose smile was bigger, Andy's or Addie's.

He loved coaxing her to try new things, even if they weren't necessarily toddler-friendly. He was all about fun, and that served as the perfect counterweight to my desire for order.

"It's okay," he'd tell me. "Everything's an experiment to her right now. Just let her do it, let her try."

That sentence runs through my head every single day. I often battle with myself as a result of having to be two parents roped into one to make sure Adalyn gets to experience what Andy would have given her, even as I strive to exert a measure of discipline that comes naturally to me. It's not easy to be something you're not, but there's really no choice when the person who originally filled that role is gone.

We were together when we saw her walk that first time, and that's a moment I'll treasure forever.

Another was Andy's final Halloween, the last holiday and last night we spent together before The Call. It was a magic night. Addie was dressed as Cinderella, with her wild static hair sticking straight up. Even though she didn't really know what was going on, there she was in her costume with a glow-up pink pumpkin in which to collect the candy she was too young to eat. It was freezing that evening, frigid for fall in Virginia, but we stayed out there for hours. We took Addie's stroller but I spent the night pushing it, like I had an invisible child, because Andy held her pretty much the entire time up on his shoulders. He toted her to every house, said "Trick or treat!" and showed Addie how to hold out her pumpkin so the candy could be properly dispensed.

The local cops were stopped at the corner of two streets handing out big blue glow sticks to all the kids. Andy insisted on getting in line so Addie could get one, even though she had no idea what a glow stick did or was. He was adamant that she should have one like all the other kids, and he finally got it for her to hold. You could see those glow sticks all the way down the street, bobbing in the grasp of kids older than Addie, seeming to light a path into the future. But the light they shed stretched only so far, just a handful of houses or maybe a block. Thinking back, the memory is metaphoric for life extending only so far, just like the light from those glow sticks. And they can flicker and fade at any time, their brightness surrendering to the darkness.

Also like life.

Addie's little hands were like icicles when we got home, but what a great night it had been, even if one not meant for a seventeen-month-old. But that was Andy. He was determined to let her have every single experience he could from the time she was a newborn.

On our walk back to our car, we were standing on the corner of Summit and Spring Streets with our group of friends, and from there we all went our separate ways. It's a moment I will never forget, a moment you think nothing of when it's happening, but now it's everything. We all waved goodbye, all of our friends scattered back to their cars, and that was the last time they saw Andy.

He left for training the next day and never came home.

CHAPTER 2

The Six Friends

I want to preface this chapter by saying that there were thousands of people who greatly impacted me the year after Andy passed. There are probably a thousand thank-you notes I still have left to write and a thousand more that I wouldn't even know the names of the people to send them to. I will never be able to put into words what that felt like and meant to me. This chapter talks about who I call "The Six Friends," but it holds a much larger meaning. It is a bigger metaphor about community, faith, and God putting you right where you need to be.

I grew up in the small town of Berryville, Virginia, in Clarke County right outside of Winchester. I started dating Andy in ninth grade at the local high school, and we remained together for all the years that followed. We were the prototype for high school sweethearts, each of us truly the other's first love. After graduating college and getting married, we ended up settling for a time in another small town called Elkton, but it never felt like home. We struggled to settle on a church and a community to be a part of.

To find the sense of community that was lacking in Elkton, when COVID hit we thought we'd move back to the Winchester area to start a family, which was where my mom and sister lived. We did not want to have children until we found the right church and village to raise our kids. Winchester, though, was an hour outside of Washington, DC, and housing prices had spiked. Thanks to cash buyers fleeing the city, those prices grew out of our comfort zone by a long shot.

Then, Andy found this house in Shenandoah County, about thirty minutes south of Winchester. He toured the house first without me and loved it but didn't think it could work with our three dogs because the yard was too small. We continued looking but couldn't find anything, so we returned to the Shenandoah County house together. I told him we could make it work. The real estate agent who originally showed Andy the house explained how amazing the Woodstock community was, and he was not wrong about this postage stamp–sized town encompassing three square miles, located along the Seven Bends of the North Fork of the Shenandoah River.

We checked out the first Lutheran church we had googled, Emanuel, and struck up an immediate relationship with the young pastor there, Pastor Nate, who was all of thirty-five years old. He gave an amazing sermon that Sunday and, even though it was COVID and everyone was wearing masks, made a point to tell us how many other young couples had been moving back to the area to raise their families. It was the kind of place nobody thinks exists anymore, a place where a former football player like Andy could work the chain crew at the local high school's home games alongside the farmers he worked with every day. I credit Andy for us finding our friend group, because getting together with strangers, whom we just met, at our pastor's house was not something I would ever do. But Andy was more outgoing and excited to go, and the rest is history.

The main street in the town's historic district was centered around the Woodstock Café, where pretty much everyone congregated, especially on Sundays when the restaurant served up an amazing brunch or on the weekends for a gourmet dinner. That's where we met up with the other young families Pastor Nate had already introduced us to. At first, there were two couples, Sam and Melissa and Josh and Amanda, who made an immediate indelible impression on us. That became the first "Friends" dinner, and it left me feeling like I was floating above the table. The conversation was pleasant and natural, and the people incredibly nice, I felt so present the entire evening. The conversations flowed effortlessly to the point I never even noticed my water glass being refilled or my food arriving at the table. I remember getting into the car that night, staring at Andy, and saying, "I think we just found our friend group here."

Melissa is an estate-planning attorney and ended up executing our will and other estate documents for us. She works in a practice with one other attorney, Rachel. Rachel and her husband Chad joined the church as well and immediately attended the next dinner. The term "The Six Friends" wasn't born until Andy's funeral, as they were the "six friends" in the family section, right where they were meant to be. Not only had we found a house we loved, we found our home and community. We found our village.

Around the same time, Andy really hit his stride working for Helena, traversing his expansive territory to check in on his numerous farming accounts, always keeping tabs and never taking anything for granted. He might have been a great salesman when it came to agricultural goods and products, but it was all genuine. He never tried to sell any customer something they didn't want or need and never took a one-size-fits-all approach, because that doesn't work when it comes to farming. Every single farm, from the smallest to the largest, is distinct and comes complete with its own set of challenges that Andy was always ready to help his customers meet. He managed two warehouses located in Winchester and Harrisonburg, and Woodstock was located smack dab in the middle of them, which made it even more perfect for us. Many of these farmers became friends. He was giddy whenever he came home after getting to see a new operation. He felt honored whenever someone allowed him onto their farm. Andy always said all he wanted was to be a reliable resource, someone people trusted and respected in the agriculture industry. And by the looks of his funeral, he was. That really was his life goal, and I feel peace knowing he reached it before he passed.

I, meanwhile, also worked in the farming industry for an agricultural lending company called Farm Credit. It was kind of strange that both of us had settled into these careers, because neither one of us had grown up on a farm. We both did, however, study agribusiness management down the road at Virginia Tech. Our young family was doing so well, I really enjoyed the opportunity my job gave me to help other families realize their dreams. My role as an underwriter left me responsible for working with people who were applying for a loan to purchase a farm or expand their current operation. I'd look at their tax returns, balance sheets, bank statements, and other financial resources to determine the relative merits of their applications. I never liked disappointing people with a negative report, but letting them bite off more than they could chew wouldn't have been good for them either. The fact is that farming isn't for the faint of heart. Some who dream of buying a farm are looking through rose-colored glasses instead of seeing things straight, and it was all too easy for the dream to become a nightmare if they were not prepared.

I mention this because it shows how Andy and I were more than a couple; we were best friends joined by genuinely common interests. I really liked working in the same industry, because it allowed us to discuss the agriculture world in a way I'm sure would have bored anyone lacking a similar interest in that culture and lifestyle.

We were doing so well we decided it was a great time to build our own home. We found the perfect tract of land in nearby Edinburg, just ten minutes away: five beautiful acres surrounded by mountain views. An idyllic place for a family to raise a bunch of kids. We settled on building a garage apartment to move into while we sold our house and built our dream home on the property. The strangest thing about that experience is I have all these pictures of Addie alone or the two of us together on our new property, but Andy isn't in a single one of them because he was too busy taking the pictures, as if those photos were the memories he wanted to leave with us after The Call. Or, maybe at some deeper intuitive level, he was planning on taking them with him.

Along the way, though, Andy fell in love with the notion of owning a farm ourselves. We ended up putting offers on multiple farms but continually found ourselves outbid. That went on for years preceding Addie and continued after she was born. At one point while I was pregnant, we found a farm we were able to enter into a Purchase and Sales agreement on and even received preapproval from the bank. All the pieces finally fell into place, but then the deal ended up falling through on the seller's side.

We were disappointed but not about to quit, and sure enough, our persistence paid off when we found a two-hundred-acre farm that checked every one of the boxes we were looking for. All we needed was preapproval from the bank and we were all set. Well, we got the preapproval letter the morning of Andy's passing on November 2, 2023. Talking about that letter, how excited he was, is the last memory I have of the life we'd built together.

"Hell yeah!" was his response, realizing the latest dream we'd hatched for our family had come true.

He couldn't have been happier, and then The Call came before we had a chance to close. I remember the lender reaching out to me the following week after the funeral.

"I just have to ask you," she said, "if Andy saw the letter before the accident."

"Yes," I reassured her, "he saw it that same morning and was absolutely over the moon."

Looking back now, I can't get over how all our previous efforts at purchasing a farm had fallen through.

"Could you imagine having a two-hundred-acre farm to manage right now on top of everything else you're going through?" our Realtor and good friend Allie asked me, weeks after the funeral.

I had never thought of things that way until she posed the question. Now, I believe there was a reason why all but one of our offers had been rejected and why we hadn't closed on the deal where our offer had been accepted. I couldn't imagine operating a farm without Andy. Call it fate, or destiny, or something that was just meant to be. Sometimes these things can't be explained.

That's when "The Six Friends" took over, supplementing the efforts of my family. They dropped everything for me and Addie. We were preparing to move at the time, and much of our lives had been packed into boxes. All of that came to a fast halt after I got The Call and quickly started moving in the opposite direction. I remember going out to my porch in those initial minutes and bawling my eyes out. I looked up to see Josh walking up the driveway and then another car pulled up, and pretty soon all my friends were there together on my porch doing their best to console me, along with my mom and sister. Because the house was all packed up, I didn't have a guest room anymore. I didn't know where anything was and had to figure out where my mom and sister could sleep that night since they didn't want to leave Addie and me alone. My brother packed up my mom's guest room and drove the contents over to my house so he could build her bed that night. Overnight, my house was transformed, functional and furnished again. And that felt strange because, on top of everything else, I was going backward.

With so many people staying at the house, we were running out of towels. Chad and Rachel ran out and got a fresh supply from Walmart, along with dinner. Little things like that, things people did without being told or asked, helped me get through those days. Whenever I needed something, it was there, like magic, because that's what people like the Six Friends coming through when you need them the most truly is.

Woodstock is a town where everybody knows everybody, and I don't think I passed a single person in a store or the street who didn't come up to hug me and offer their condolences in the weeks that followed. Andy had touched so many people in our time there, and all of them had their own memories of him. I had never met many of the people, but they all knew Andy, and they shared stories about him I had never heard before. I knew he had this great big personality that could fill a room, yet until then, I'm not sure I fully grasped how many people were actually squeezed into that room.

And he kept touching them even after the funeral. So many people sent flowers that we didn't know what do with them all. We ended up distributing the bouquets all around town, gave them to local businesses like the Woodstock Café and the nursing homes beyond the town center. For weeks, everywhere you went, Andy's flowers greeted you, peering out from storefront windows. And that's just the way Andy would have wanted it, a little bit of him spread throughout the town, bringing color and happiness to all those who passed by.

In the darkest moments of life, it's nice to spot rays of sunshine peeking through the clouds.

CHAPTER 3

The Expedition

Sunday, four days after the accident, my mom, my sister, and my sister's husband accompanied me to the Richmond trauma center to pick up Andy. A hearse from the funeral home met us there, and I also met Andy's commanding officer, Lieutenant Colonel Hall, whose call had changed my life forever.

He was in uniform and had the straight back, strong features, and stoic demeanor you'd expect from an army officer. He gave me the tightest hug I'd ever felt, and as we separated, his legs buckled and he sank to his knees. I had already caught wind of the fact that his initial call, and the one that followed from the surgeon giving me the news I already knew, represented a breach of military protocol. Apparently, procedure dictated that the army still notify the immediate families of deceased soldiers in person with that dreaded knock on the door or ring of the bell.

"I know you might be in trouble for what you did," I told him at one point, "but I am very glad I found out the way I did. Otherwise, I might not have known for hours that Andy was gone."

Hall swallowed hard. "I did what I would want done if it were my wife."

After retrieving Andy's body from the medical examiner's office, we followed the hearse to the funeral home in Edinburg in the Ford Expedition Max that Andy bought me to fit the big family we were never going to have now. My brother-in-law Trae was driving, and we were trailed by Andy's brothers and their wives, a few friends who'd made the trip with me, including some of Andy's Helena friends who joined the procession along the way, as well as Scott, the Casualty and Affairs officer assigned to me. I figured the ride home would prove as solemn and uneventful as the ride there.

I was wrong.

Our small procession was led by the white funeral home hearse with green markings. The first overpass we drove under should have given me a hint of what was to come. I glanced up from an incoming text and spotted a fire engine with an American flag draped over its side parked in full view, a trio of uniformed firefighters holding fast to salute as we approached.

This is for Andy, I realized. *This is for us.*

What a wonderful gesture, I thought, warmed and moved by it before returning to the text that had just come in.

Then, a few miles down, another overpass appeared and, atop it, another fire engine, this one with its ladder raised and maybe a dozen uniformed firefighters, centered over a massive American flag hanging down over the railing, saluting too. The sight was awe-inspiring, mesmerizing, and so emotionally wrenching. I smiled, even as I couldn't stop from tearing up.

I held my gaze on that overpass until it shrank from view out the Expedition's rear window, touched by the kindness of strangers and wishing only that I'd had the foresight to snap a picture of that incredible sight.

As it turned out, I'd get plenty more chances.

I could see the next overpass coming up in the distance and what appeared to be tiny figurines standing before a toy fire truck. Drawing closer, I spotted yet another American flag, this time hanging higher from the railing, held there by a pair of firefighters in dress uniforms saluting with their free hands. They were joined by civilians who had either accompanied them there or joined in on their own—men, women, children, and even toddlers little older than Addie saluting too.

It turned out Josh, with the immense help from many others, helped arrange the whole thing. I had called him when I found out we were bringing Andy home and asked if he could organize a small homecoming on Main Street for friends and family. I hadn't expected a homecoming that spanned the entire two-and-a-half-hour-drive home. Josh was a volunteer firefighter in Woodstock, so he knew the right people to call at the various municipalities' fellow departments that lined Route 64 and then, later, Route 81. His wife, Amanda, arranged for a professional photographer and videographer so that Andy's final ride home would be preserved forever, mainly for Addie to watch one day when she's old enough to appreciate it.

We passed under around thirty-five overpasses along the way, and firefighters maintained a stoic, reserved, and respectful presence on almost every one of them. These were American heroes themselves, paying tribute to a fallen soldier and fellow hero. It wasn't just the overpasses that were crowded either. People had pulled off the highway onto the shoulder of the road and were saluting us as we passed. I could not believe the multitude of strangers who paid their respects along the way.

Speaking of which, training my focus ahead in anticipation of the next overpass spared me a sight that would have affected me in an entirely different way. The extended training weekend that started so tragically on Thursday ended on this day, and Andy's unit was returning home at the same time as our procession. Passing a line of Humvees driving on the other side of the highway left everyone in my car holding their breath, afraid I'd notice and make the unavoidable conclusion. But I didn't. They rolled on, and so did we.

One of the men in Andy's unit, Mike, happened to also be a police officer in Richmond. He reached out to me on Facebook days before the procession and offered to lead it from Richmond. He was there when we arrived at the medical examiner's office and led us onto I-95. From there, local and state police took over from one another at regular intervals in guiding us along I-95 at the beginning of the trip. At one point, they closed off access to the highway to allow us an unimpeded merge up the ramp so the small line of vehicles could cling together.

"This is what they do for the president," my brother-in-law remarked.

No one forewarned me about any of this, wanting it all to be a surprise, a pleasant shock in stark contrast to the one I was greeted with on Thursday afternoon. That was especially true of one of the last tributes we passed under: a giant American flag suspended between two cranes over Route 81, flanked and fronted by ordinary people who wanted to show their support with a wave, a salute, a sign, or just a smile. I wish we could have stopped to give me the opportunity to thank every single one of them who had shown up out of the goodness of their hearts.

Closer to Woodstock, to home, the overpasses and the mouth-dropping ceremonies carried out atop them came to an end, replaced by something equally inspiring.

Farm equipment was parked on the side of the outer edges of Route 81 all along the thirty-five-mile route between Harrisonburg and Woodstock. And this wasn't ordinary farming machinery or random farmers—they were Andy's customers, the pieces lined up on the side of the road enabling these humble men Andy considered his friends to pay their proper respects to him.

Through the whole of this experience, the compassion people showed purely of their own volition impressed me beyond measure. I didn't know their politics and, sometimes, even their names. I didn't know who they voted for, what teams they rooted for, and had no idea of their dreams and ambitions, their own failures and successes, tragedies and celebrations. But to see their tractors, pickers, backhoes, loaders, cultivators, and balers lined up one after the other for as far as the eye could see made for an indescribable feeling. And before those machines stood the men and women who worked them: farmers, Andy's customers whom he treated like family returning that favor with a show of affection that was both genuine and organic, standing in sad stoicism with a salute or a wave, while also standing as testament to the power of the human spirit. People so often surprise you, often for the worse but in this case so much for the better.

We had set out for Richmond in the bright sunshine of the early morning, a roughly two-and-half-hour drive. It would take us four hours to get home, thanks to the endless memorial displays of tribute.

I wish it had stretched on forever.

Our police escort guided us slowly along Main Street in Woodstock en route to the funeral home in Edinburg. The parade of love, respect, and support that had begun on highway overpasses, then continued with endless roadside displays, culminated here in our hometown to an even more dramatic and uplifting effect.

My neighbors stood lining the roadside, on their porches, or in their front yards waving those souvenir American flags attached to a stick. It looked like the Fourth of July, the outpouring of love and friendship overwhelming. Pastor Nate stood with one foot in the road and the other on the sidewalk, crying as he proudly held the Emanuel Church flag overhead, the flag that had welcomed us to Woodstock years before. It felt so long ago now. A measure of the football team was packed into the back of a stake-bed truck, their gold-and-blue Falcon jerseys shining in the sun.

For some reason in that moment, my mind flashed back to some of the truly important things Andy had squeezed into his final months, checkmarks placed next to the items on his bucket list. It was a lifelong dream of his, for instance, to attend a New England Patriots game at Gillette Stadium in Foxborough, Massachusetts. The tickets came courtesy of a major account he had that promised him tickets if he reached certain sales goals. He exceeded those goals and didn't waste a second reminding the supplier about the tickets he was promised. We piggybacked our trip to New England with a Helena meeting he had in Maine. Addie was only four months old at the time, and my mother came with us to serve as babysitter. We had such a great time, even though the Patriots lost.

Andy loved the team, thanks to the area being one of the ten stops his family made through his youth to accommodate his father's transfers in the military. He inherited the obsession from his older brother Adam, and his go-to radio stop in the many long drives he made in his truck was a SiriusXM Patriots podcast twelve months a year. As great a time as we had at Gillette Stadium, since The Call, whenever the Patriots are on television, I can't watch. But I'm going to buy Addie a little Patriots jersey, because I know that's what Andy would have done, so she could wear it when he took her to a game. So I'll take her instead. I'm going to channel Andy and do the things with her he would have loved to do.

As for the items on Andy's bucket list that can't be completed, like camping and bareback horse riding in Montana and visiting London, I'm going to check those off for him too. Doing the things he so wanted to do himself will be one of my ways of honoring him, of preserving our relationship in that way. And when Addie's old enough, I hope she'll accompany me so we can check some of those things off together.

Just like Andy would have wanted.

CHAPTER 4

The Boots

It rained the following Friday, the day of Andy's funeral. My sisters-in-law, Caylee and Lauren, ordered several black dresses in toddler sizes for Adalyn from Amazon. And all I could think of, watching her spinning around and dancing happily in the one I selected for her, was that you don't want to put your seventeen-month-old in a black dress for any reason. I watched her do that and was struck by the reality that our little girl had no idea what was happening. And thank God for that.

I was in the passenger seat of our Expedition Max, driven again by my brother-in-law Trae, with Addie directly behind me in her car seat and my mother seated next to her. Five years ago, not long after I turned twenty-two, I had been sitting in that very same seat when my father passed suddenly, an irony that wasn't lost on me. Trae was behind the wheel on that day as well, with Andy seated in the front passenger seat. And my mom, sister, and I were holding the urn with my dad's ashes inside in the backseat. Here we were again, headed front row to a funeral, with another family member not in the car. When Addie started asking where he was, I'd tell her that "Dada's in the sky," so I guess my dad was up there too. I thought then that I was too young to lose a parent, at an age where many were dealing with the losses of their grandparents instead. At least, though, I had all those years of memories to comfort me, while all Addie really had was the picture of her and Andy she hugged every night before bed.

Andy's funeral rekindled memories of my dad dying suddenly. I was too young to lose a father and now much too young to lose a husband. But I wasn't thinking of the bad things, the shock and dawning reality of Andy's death. I was focused instead on doing his life justice and making the day perfect for him. I wanted this to be what I knew Andy would have wanted: a celebration of life, not a dark affair defined by anguish and misery. That's not who Andy was and not how I wanted the people who loved him the most to remember him. I wanted them to remember Andy for exactly who and what he was. There would be time for grief, anger, and all the what-ifs later. As far as that first week leading up to the funeral, though, I didn't have time to be angry.

I had worn a pair of cowgirl boots to our wedding and wore the very same pair for Andy's funeral, as well as his visitation the previous night. People may not have noticed me wearing mine, but they couldn't miss Andy's pair on display at the visitation and the funeral too.

It just felt right, since we had spent so much time that week ruminating on all the fields he'd walked in those boots, the many, many miles he'd put on the soles like tire treads. It ended up morphing into a movement where those closest to Andy all wore boots to his funeral. His brother Adam wore his all week to break them in and was like, "These things suck. They're not even comfortable."

His weren't broken in as well as ours. And at the funeral I walked down the aisle exactly as I did on our wedding day, only this time, instead of my soon-to-be husband, I walked toward Andy's coffin draped in an American flag and climbed the stairs to the podium to address the assembled standing-room-only crowd. I looked down at his coffin and thought about how I had honored the vow 'til death do us part literally, sharing this one final moment with him, wearing the same boots to celebrate his life that I'd worn to celebrate our lives together.

I was one of many to speak inside an assembly hall at the fairgrounds that were practically right next to our home just off Route 81. Woodstock is such a small town that the whole day of the funeral took place within the two-mile radius from my house to the Emanuel Lutheran Church where the procession gathered for the short ride to the funeral. There is something gently comforting in that, making it feel as if the whole of it encompassed home. The town, the church, and those fairgrounds indistinguishable from one another.

There's a lot I remember with crystal clarity from that day, but nothing greater than the speakers who climbed the stairs to the podium one after the other to offer their memories of Andy in voices cracking with emotion and breaking with grief. I was hearing some of the stories for the first time and listening to well-worn ones with a new appreciation that made them feel fresh and new because they were coming from the voices of those I'd shared Andy with who loved him too. Each in their own way.

First up was Andy's commanding officer in the Army Reserve, Lieutenant Colonel Aaron Hall.

"I had the honor of being Andy's battalion commander," he began. "I've spent the last week reviewing every email, text, and phone call from the past year and a half, our entire relationship as men, as husbands, as fathers, soldiers, and as commanders together. Andy started his career as an SMP (Simultaneous Membership Program that combines ROTC with the Army Reserve) cadet assigned to the 2nd of the 317th where he shadowed NCOs and officers who are charged with training and educating soldiers about what it means to be in the army.

"Being an SMP cadet is not a requirement. It's something that cadets do to gain more on-the-job training before they commission as an officer. Andy stepped up to the challenge, happy, eager and willing to lean in and take charge. He never said, 'I'm just a cadet.' He worked to get better every day and to learn from his NCOs.

"His first assignment as platoon leader was the 639th Transportation Company. Andy displayed an exceptional ability to connect with soldiers through challenging and realistic training. He positively impacted his team and fellow officers with his charisma and technical abilities. His leadership was recognized by the battalion, and he was selected to lead the transportation section of our support operation cell. He led the unit through Operation Blueridge Resolve, overseeing a team of soldiers moving over three hundred million dollars of equipment and ensuring the deployability of the battalion headquarters. He accepted the challenge as a lieutenant and quickly made an impact. Andy was selected from amongst his peers and amongst many that outranked him to command the 275th Quartermaster Company. His ability to navigate hard situations, maintain composure, and produce results is unmatched in our formation. It was in this position with the 275th that I met Andy."

Listening to Commander Hall, it occurred to me that Andy wasn't mine alone. I had shared him with so many others who loved him in a different way but loved him all the same. I always knew that the Andy I loved wasn't just that way for me; sitting there in my cowgirl boots listening to the speakers, I realized just how expansive his reach was.

"He'd combine words like *yessir*. Laughing, hugging, and just in general bringing light into the room. After our meeting, I pulled Andy aside, looked at him, and said, 'I have something hard to tell you, but I need to be honest.' I said, 'Man, you're the worst commander I have for twenty-eight days out of the month, but I'll be darned if you aren't the best one I have for the two days I have you. How do we go about fixing that ratio?' The point wasn't lost on him. It was just reality. I honestly believe that's because he could make a difference, and everyone wanted more of him. He could be ready at the drop of a hat, transition, listen, and focus on the task in front of him and execute. He was the epitome of a combat leader: smart, agile, deliberate when needed, but decisive at the crucial moment. I would have gone to war with him any day. That's the Andy I'll always keep in my heart, and I cherish that memory of him.

"People are put in our lives at very crucial times. I know that Andy was put in mine to teach me about compassion. He helped me regain my sense of humor in times of stress. He taught me to love my family hard and that sometimes things don't have to be perfect to still be good. I've always had a fire in my belly for the army, for hard training, for standing shoulder to shoulder. Last Thursday night took a bit of that fire away. I don't know when it will come back, but I know it will. Andy's legacy will live on within our formation, the soldiers he fought to promote, the soldiers that get up early to run based off his example, the soldiers that put on their boots when the nation calls because they live by the same values that Andy showed us every day. He's a part of my fire."

Part of the Military Honors tradition is that at the funeral, the family is presented with the flag that had been draped over the coffin prior to burial. That, though, presented a challenge because we weren't actually burying Andy that day. He and I had been too young to even purchase burial plots, and I was very undecided on where to lay him to rest. Not only that, Andy wanted to be cremated.

Absent the burial, the Army folded up the flag displayed on his coffin and fit another in its place. Normally at a military funeral, the deceased soldier would go straight into the ground to the playing of "Taps" and a twenty-one-gun salute. On this day, all of that transpired before the coffin went right back into the hearse, covered in that fresh flag, instead of into the ground.

Technically, Andy had suffered a line-of-duty death, but I didn't feel I deserved to get the ceremonial folded flag that comes with that. It wasn't like Andy had died in Afghanistan or Iraq, or served this long military career overseas, and I still struggle with the notion of considering myself a military spouse. I don't want to compare myself, or others to compare me, to widows with a husband deployed in a war zone who learned he wasn't coming home. To be clear, I felt like Andy deserved the sanctimony and ritual of this day due to all of his hard work and sacrifice. But I didn't feel like I did, leaving me to experience one of my many identity crises I would be faced with as I was handed the folded flag.

What had my life just become?

The army actually provided three flags: one for me, a second for Adalyn, and a third I gave to Andy's Uncle Wayne, because his parents hadn't come to the funeral.

They hadn't come to our wedding either.

They were estranged from Andy's life and weren't there for the most celebratory parts of it, like his high school and college graduations, or even the birth of a granddaughter they had never seen. Before he died, my dad had become a father figure to Andy. And there was a point prior to Andy's passing when he reached out to his parents to try and salvage their relationship. I don't know how to fully reconcile that, because it makes utterly no sense to me—I don't think Andy was fully reconciled to it either, although he had no choice but to accept it.

I celebrated with Andy when he was promoted to captain just a week prior to his death but, otherwise, had no idea about all the commendations and awards he had received, including being up for one of the highest awards you can get in the army without going to war. I had never known any of this until the visitation the night before, when Commander Hall presented me with all the awards Andy had already received. And, somehow, I felt like I didn't deserve them because I hadn't even known. It felt wrong for anyone but Andy to possess these well-earned awards he'd been too humble to tell me about. He was the one who earned them, not me.

Somehow, it made perfect sense that so much of this goes back to having parents who were never really engaged with all his achievements, never there with a celebratory hug or pat on the back through his late-teen and adult years. Andy liked tangibles because they told him he was doing a good job, words he wished he heard from his parents over the years. The problem with that is you might think hearing the equivalent of "good job" from getting an award, a promotion, or a commendation, from Helena or the military, would provide the same kind of satisfaction. But it was never enough, because you're forever waiting to hear it from your dad or mom. Maybe that's why Andy never shared his many accolades with me, because I wasn't the one he desperately sought approval from.

I know a lot of his determination to be the greatest father he could be, to prioritize that over everything else, was about giving Addie what he'd never had. There are no tangibles in fatherhood. No commemorative awards or distinguished honors. In this case, Addie laughing or smiling or putting her little basketball through her tiny hoop in the living room was all Andy needed. These were the equivalent of our young daughter saying "good job" to her dad in her own way before she could even speak.

I had not seen or spoken to Andy's parents since high school. When I first heard about the accident and called Andy's brother Adam, I asked him if he could tell his parents. He got on the phone with them, and they dropped everything and rushed to the trauma center in Richmond from our hometown of Berryville. That eats me alive because, in one sense, it feels like they were there for him when I wasn't. In another sense, though, where had they been for the rest of his life? They showed up when there was nothing they could do for him, but they weren't a part of his life when there was plenty they could have done.

I almost feel bad for them, sad anyway, since they missed out on so much good. I had a house full of people bringing me food and friendship, while they returned to Berryville alone, grieving the loss of their son with nobody there for them, because they had alienated their entire family. The contrast was striking, highlighting the importance of community. I could never have gotten through this alone. That's not an accident, it's not luck. A community is something Andy and I built for ourselves. At one point, I asked his brothers to go and see his parents before the funeral. I wanted them to know that they were welcome, no matter what transpired in the past. They sent flowers and ordered a tree in his memory but failed to show up.

"In the days since Andy's passing, people have said how wonderful this community has been to embrace Amy and Addie," Virginia State Senator Timmy French said from the podium at the service, picking up where Lieutenant Colonel Hall had left off, "but really Amy and Andy embraced this community. I am a better person for having known Andy King. If you take anything away from what I've said today, it's to be like Andy. Put a smile on your face, like Andy did. Give back to your community, like Andy did. Work hard, like Andy did. Make sure things are better for yourself and for someone else, like Andy did."

Timmy and Andy had been great friends. The French family would do anything for us and have supported and protected me ever since Andy's passing. Andy worked with Timmy on their farm and ran the chains with him at the football games. He was elected to the Virginia state senate the Tuesday after Andy died. Nothing would have pleased Timmy more than getting a celebratory hug from Andy after his victory. That's the kind of hole you can never fill, but I can't say it didn't feel comforting to know others felt Andy's loss, in their own way, as deeply and profoundly as I did. I shared so much of him in life, and now I was sharing him in death. And what continued to strike me through the course of all the speeches and all the tears was the profound effect Andy had on so many lives.

"He watched the sun rise through the windshield of his pickup truck so he could get out in the field," Timmy continued. "Make that eight a.m. meeting and get back in the truck and do it again in the next county over. Farmers aren't quick to change. They are stuck in their ways. What I'm saying is, if I have a hat on, I stand behind it. Before Andy, there wasn't a Helena hat in this valley. Now there's hats, shirts, sweatshirts, and even the occasional jacket. One thing I'd like to say about his work ethic is that he crossed hurdles that he didn't even know were there. He broke barriers that he didn't even know existed. He did that by just being himself. When others said, 'Why would I do that?' Andy said, 'Why not?'"

The next speaker was Sean Duff, a good friend and sales rep for Helena who worked with Andy in the same office.

"Beyond his family, Andy loved two things: corn and winning. Most days were a competition between him and our suppliers, other Helena salesmen, our boss, but mostly between him and himself. He was always striving to get better and use every resource to his advantage, demanding the best from everyone, including himself, and accepting nothing less in return. At Helena, we have an awards banquet every year, and Andy wanted to win all of those awards. And he did not hesitate to let people know who were voting that he wanted them all. He won a few, but the one he wanted to win the most was Location of the Year, the award given to the most outstanding Helena branch, because he wanted to share that glory with others, knowing that he had built the best team. Last year, Andy and his branch won that award. It was the first time any of us had ever seen him speechless. We had countless conversations over the last four years where Andy would say, 'We have to do more. Let's do it better and bigger.' He woke up every morning with something to prove, never willing to settle for good enough."

Listening to those speeches drove home the fact of how much I shared Andy with others, not only the military but also Helena. He had the career of a lifetime in only five years, eight if you include the three years he interned for the company while an undergraduate at Virginia Tech. Very few people actually love their work, especially in their twenties when they're just getting started. Andy loved every part of his job, couldn't wait to get out the door in the morning to start a day that often didn't end until the sun went down around seven or eight o'clock at night. He was working farmer's hours, you might say, while I was taking care of everything at home. Everybody wanted so much of him, and I think, deep down, I resented how it took him away from Addie and me. I had gone from dealing with my dad's sudden passing to getting married, to having our daughter, to then facing Andy's death just a month after I had finally gone back to work. Through all the stories and anecdotes, through the long week leading up to this service, I learned exactly who Andy was.

But who was I?

CHAPTER 5

Dada's in the Sky

A therapist I went to see about how to handle a parent's death with a child advised me that you need to be very blunt. *He's not coming home. Mommy will be coming home tonight, but Daddy's never coming home.*

I followed that advice, to which Addie would ask me, "But where is he?"

I would point to the sky and say, "Dada's in the sky."

And it stuck. Every single time we went outside, she pointed up at the sky and said, "Dada! Dada's in the sky!"

Taking that a step further, when we say our prayers at night, we'll say, "Thank you, God. Thank you for Mommy, thank you for Auntie, thank you for Grammy." We go through everyone and Addie says, on her own, "Thank you for Dada."

To which I add, "In heaven. Thank you, God, for being with Dada in heaven."

So now, when Addie says, "Dada's in the sky," she'll add, "in heaven with God."

She's starting to catch on to the notion of a family unit at day care, because she can see the other kids have moms *and* dads. And she'll ask me, "Where's my dad at?"

"Some daddies watch their babies from the ground," I tell her, "and other daddies watch their babies from up in the sky. Your daddy's watching you from the sky. He can see you but you can't see him."

She nods and accepts that because that's her normal, compared to the other kids for whom two parents are normal. I tell her she still has a daddy too. She just can't see hers like the other kids can.

Separation anxiety, meanwhile, is normal for toddlers, but I began to notice it was becoming more exaggerated with Addie when I left her because I was her only parent. Her other parent, after all, left one day and didn't come back. So, whenever I left her with a babysitter or dropped her off at day care, I started making a point to say something like, "I'll be back tonight," or "I'll pick you up later." People are always telling me to try and sneak out of the room when I am leaving her to avoid the meltdown. I refuse to do it, though, because it isn't fair to her to sneak away and not say goodbye. Her pediatrician said this was normal developmental stuff, but I kept asking myself what normal was for Addie. Is this part of a greater anxiety developing? Is my child struggling and I'm not doing enough to help her?

That's why kissing that photo of Andy remained a part of her nightly bedtime ritual. It brought her joy and helped her feel his presence, keeping his memory alive. I've watched Addie develop a new relationship with Andy, just as I have. In addition to the 5K I started planning in his honor, I've created an agricultural scholarship in his name. Those are the happy parts of grief that keep me going because I'm not harping on the accident, how it happened, and how he died. I'm focusing on things I can do to create a new relationship with him.

And I did the same with Addie. If the birds were singing, I'd say, "That's Dada saying hi through the birds." When we found a feather, I'd say, "It's a gift from Dada!" When it thundered outside, I'd say, "That's Dada in the sky!" And every time she spotted an American flag, she would point and say, "That's Dada's flag!" with a big smile on her face. I made everything as much about Andy for her as I could, because it provided an outlet to talk about him and to remember him. As time has moved forward and her language has developed, I am able to tell her more stories about Andy that she understands. She now tells people, "My dada grows corn…for the cows!"

It is almost like I'm creating an ethereal version of Andy, because there's nothing left of him here. And that brought me back to the experience of losing my own father. I was twenty-two at the time and it hurt just as much, only in a different way.

My dad took his life three months after Andy and I got married.

It was almost a relief, because his life had been riddled by addiction for so long. His downfall started after he broke his back when I was in middle school. He put off surgery as long as he could but ultimately had no choice and got hooked on the painkiller Percocet in the aftermath. I was thirteen years old, and by the time I was old enough to realize the extent of his sickness, it had progressed so badly that we'd expect bad news every time the phone rang. I had found my dad blue on the floor many times when I got home from school, been picked up from practices by him drunk, had watched him have two withdrawal seizures, and worried about him every day of my life since the start of his addiction. I had always known my dad would drink himself to death or have some kind of accident and had been grieving him for years. Suicide though, I never expected. My dad was the best father ever when he was sober, but when his addiction was rampant, he was someone I did not recognize.

It wasn't that he didn't try. He had a successful thirty-day stint in rehab and followed that up by committing himself to the Twelve-Step Program. Sobriety stuck for varying periods at a time, but then he'd relapse. I found myself so angry at him because I'd think, *Who wants to be like this??Who wants to drink himself to death?* He was sick, and the truth is sober he was a terrific father, but it wasn't often enough for those last nine years or so.

I always figured that when the inevitable call came, it would be to tell me what I'd long been expecting, that he drank himself to death. Suicide came out of nowhere. It shocked all of us.

Strangely, he was sober the whole week before he died. He was texting my sister and me Bible verses.

"Girls," he told us, "I'm gonna take care of myself, I'm gonna beat this."

Then the next day he was gone.

It's funny, but more recently my memories of my dad have become fonder. He was always so upbeat, positive, and encouraging, even when he was masking his addictions. His solution to everything was "Life's too short. Do what makes you happy. And when it stops making you happy, stop doing it." He was always my biggest supporter, the person I could call who'd make me feel better no matter how down I was. He was a boater, and I have so many happy memories of our family out on the water in the bay every single weekend of the summer.

There were signs even through his optimism, though, that something was off. He'd encourage me to quit my job just because I was having a hard day. "Go make yourself happy, no matter what the consequences, no matter what the cost is," he'd say. That might have been what I needed to hear to feel better in the moment, but it's not really sage advice. He could be so irrational and yet loving at the same time. I can't say Andy's death has made me miss him more, just the good parts of him when the alcohol wasn't winning. He was working as a Realtor when Andy and I were looking for our first house. Not only did he find us the perfect starter home in Elkton, he gave us his commission to apply toward the down payment. I know my dad tried, and I take solace in the fact there were some good times sprinkled in among a wider swath of the bad.

That didn't change the fact I was attending Al-Anon meetings, a support group for the family and friends of people affected by alcoholism, when I was seventeen. There were nights back then when I'd call Andy, who was dealing with his own issues at home, and say something like, "My dad's drunk, and he's going crazy downstairs." Andy would say, "Stay on the phone with me." And many nights I'd fall asleep with the phone pressed against my ear.

Andy was with me through all of it, the only person in the world who truly understood that part of my life. And his death drove home the realization that nobody ever again will know all there is to know about me, and that's been a big part of my grief. My father was that person and then Andy was, and now they're both gone. My father was with me through so much, and Andy was with me through the rest, including my dad's funeral. When Andy died, obviously, I didn't have either one of them and never would again.

The worst thing about grief is realizing its permanence. I remember looking at a picture after Andy's funeral of just my dad and Andy and thinking, *Wow, no one in this photo exists anymore*. Things will get better, sure, but you'll never have that person in your life again. You can't. The best way I can describe the feeling is panic. You need and want something so bad, but it's impossible to find and there is no replacement. You become a prisoner to these feelings.

It was so important to both Andy and me to have this big family full of love, big enough to fit in the Ford Expedition Max he bought me with that expectation in mind. I know if something happened to me, I wouldn't have wanted it to just be Andy and Adalyn. She'd need a mother figure in her life, just like she will need a father figure at some point outside of her uncles, because there's a huge difference in that father figure living under the same roof. It's got to be the right person, and good luck to them coming into this sense of community swarming around me. They're just going to have to be an awesome freaking person. I say that all the time, but even if that person exists, I know I'll still want to continue breaking all the generational trauma Andy and I both suffered. I had planned to do it alongside him and feel duty-bound to the same commitment without him. And if I meet someone else, I'm still going to share the experiences with Adalyn that Andy would have wanted to have, like taking her to a New England Patriots game dressed in her little Patriots jersey.

For a while, I got very emotional when Adalyn started crying after I dropped her off at day care. Well, almost every child cries when they get dropped off and then five minutes after you drive away, they're smiling. But I couldn't shake the feeling that I was leaving my child in emotional distress. Rationally, I knew I'm wasn't, but reason didn't apply when I was crying too and had to force myself to drive away.

It makes me think ahead to momentous experiences Addie has looming, like her first day of kindergarten. That will be a big one, and I plan on having an entire entourage there to drop her off. My family, Andy's brothers, my friends—she'll be the kid who has a lot more support than just a mom and dad. I don't want her to focus on what she doesn't have but on what she does. She's going to travel with a village. I know none of that will ever replace Andy, but Addie will know she's loved and supported. And she'll be aware that if she's having this problem she can call Uncle Alex, and if she's having that problem she can call Uncle Adam, and so on.

But another challenge awaited, that being the move to the new property we'd purchased. Andy and I had plans to build a house and live in a garage apartment while we waited for it to be finished on that beautiful stretch of land we'd both fallen in love with. After The Call, I changed the garage apartment to basically be a small home instead. There was no point in building a larger house anymore.

I really worried about us leaving our home in Woodstock and Addie thinking, *How's Dada going to find us? Are we leaving him?* With the passage of time, though, the massive delay in construction became a blessing, because Addie had reached a point where I didn't think she expected Andy to walk in the door. So I felt good about sticking with the plan, while ensuring that we took Andy with us. There would be a shelf in her room to keep the folded flag she got at the funeral, and her favorite photo would hang on the wall outside her bedroom so she could still hug and kiss Dada before bed every night and he would be a part of our new home. I wanted Addie to remember and always love him, without doing anything to make her think Andy was coming back. And I took comfort in being aware that Andy knew where we were going to be, because we'd picked out the land together.

It turned out to be fortuitous that we hadn't selected anything for the house yet. That enabled me to choose the tile, the flooring, and the paint colors, showing them to Addie in advance so she felt a part of the process. It may not be the house that Andy built, yet it rested upon land he loved.

To be honest, I started reflecting on this a lot, because I knew how difficult closing the door to our house in Woodstock for the last time would be. It was the door we brought our daughter through when we came home from the hospital, as well as the door that Andy walked out one day and never came back, the door I walked through to sit on my porch after I got The Call.

I knew moving would prove to be a good idea. Our house felt heavy without Andy, and I was starting to feel ready for the change. Everyday tasks like cooking, even just being in the kitchen or sitting down in the same chair where I was when the phone rang, drained me. That's what I mean by heavy, and it's why I didn't plan to take a single piece of furniture in the move, especially that chair.

You'll never move on, but you have to move forward. I don't get hung up with leaving all of Andy's things exactly as he left them. Some people may, and that's fine if it makes them feel better, but it wasn't for me. Accepting the new life helps honor the one I lost.

None of that will bring Andy back, and packing up his stuff has helped me accept my new reality. Just like taking off my wedding ring early on. I was conflicted about doing that. But I think it was important to do, because my bare finger is a reminder that I am not married anymore and Andy is not here. He was never going to be the last of anything, because I'm still young and firmly believe that you can move forward and hold on at the same time. Those two things are not mutually exclusive. And I can still love and cherish Andy without his toothbrush sitting on the ledge of the sink.

People tell you, "Don't make any big decisions or rash changes within the first year." That's the most common refrain you hear when you're grieving. Maybe that's true generally, but it wasn't for me. If there was such a thing as a rulebook with timelines in it, I would have thrown it out the window. I didn't want to be sitting in the same house next Christmas waiting with Addie for Santa to show up without Andy. I want to make our own Christmas memories in our new house. I'm not afraid of change, not after so much of it has been forced upon me.

It comes down to instinct. I trust mine, and I trust that Andy approves of everything I'm doing. A house is just a wooden structure laid over a concrete foundation, and Andy doesn't live there anymore.

But he will live forever in our hearts.

PART TWO

THE GIFT TIME GIVES US

How do I say the words I want to
You're not here to hear them.
All these words held in my chest, you
Left before I freed them.

If I look out and shout, is
There some small chance they'll get through?
Could I yell them, could I whisper, if I
Try hard enough, they'll reach you.

I'd tell you that I miss you, and
I wish you were around, I,
I can't help but think I failed to
Say more often how I'm proud.

Maybe I could write them
On a page, and make them real.
Would written words allow then
The rest of us to feel?

I'd write about the memories;
What connected you to us.
Write the moments and the journeys,
And never let them rust.

Right here in this moment,
I think I'll use them both.
I'll speak these words I've written,
Words I need to say the most.

Could I have tried harder, or

Should I have maybe pushed?
Put more determined effort
Into something overlooked.

My mind is full of maybes,
Why's, and or's, and if's.
Can't help myself but blame me for
Taking granted old time's gift.

You never needed my approval
Only ever your own
But I have felt in all these people
You made your place amongst their own.

I promise, I'll always foster, and
I'll love all of those you chose.
Even more so wife and daughter,
The two souls you loved the most.

I hope I said all I needed to
I hope you heard it
I hope you heard all you needed to
I hope you know you deserved it.

Now I've said the words I need to,
And you're still here to hear them.
I hope you're always with me, and
I hope to feel you feel them.

Alex King
(reprinted with permission)

CHAPTER 6

Peekaboo!

Andy wasn't big on "stuff." He wasn't a hoarder, didn't really collect sports memorabilia other than the New England Patriots jerseys that hung in his closet. But after The Call, I checked the Notes function on his iPhone to find some passwords I needed.

It made for a strange experience. On the one hand, I felt like I was invading his privacy. On the other, I was struck by the eerie sensation that he wasn't gone at all, as if the phone magically brought him back to life, since the content of his emails and texts were pure Andy. Notes apparently was the repository where he tucked all the plans he'd laid out for Adalyn for years to come. She was to start gymnastics at the age of three and soccer at four, according to his research. He researched everything we could sign her up for. And he even notated date night ideas for the two of us and Christmas gift ideas for me. Andy might have been a spur-of-the-moment guy, but he was clearly thinking ahead in areas I wasn't thinking about at all.

I read those notes over and over again, until they felt old and I was no longer roiled by the sense that Andy was still here. Not that I wouldn't welcome any sign of his presence, and I'm pretty certain I received one around the same time.

I don't think I slept for one second the night of November 2. I remember putting Addie to bed and sitting on the couch with my mom and sister repeating out loud, "I can't believe this is happening." People showed up to my house all through the night, even through the early morning hours. No one knew what to do, except drive from wherever they were in the world to end up on my front porch.

The night of November 3, though, may have been worse. By ten o'clock everyone had trickled out of the house except for my mom, sister, and best friend Lydia. I remember taking Benadryl just to fall asleep and everyone whispering about how I needed to sleep and eat. I went to bed for a few hours and woke up in the middle of the night to Adalyn screaming. I walked out of my bedroom and found my mom, sister, and daughter all crying. Adalyn was struggling to sleep, and my sister Nicole and mom had been trying to get her down for hours and were totally at a loss. Adalyn definitely sensed something was very wrong in our lives. I told my mom and Nicole to go to sleep and let me take a turn. I turned off all the lights, sat down on a chair in the living room, and lay back with Adalyn facing out, her back against my stomach and head on my chest as I held her tight and tearfully prayed for her to settle.

All of a sudden, she sat up. Her wailing stopped, and she started playing peekaboo out toward the living room away from me. No one was playing with her—at least no one I could see, but that didn't stop her from giggling and laughing. And it wasn't a transitory thing; she went on playing for a couple of minutes.

I truly wonder if it was Andy, showing her, and probably me too, that he was okay and watching over us. Like it was his way of helping me settle her. We've all heard the stories about kids having imaginary friends until the age of five or so, but I don't think Addie was imagining someone playing peekaboo with her. I believe with all my heart it was Andy, and just because I couldn't see him doesn't mean he wasn't there. Dada might be in the sky now, but he was capable, at least that one time, of popping in long distance.

My mom stayed with me for a few months after the funeral. That allowed me to grieve and Addie to get to know her "Grammy" even better. Of course, she never got to meet her grandpa, because my dad passed more than three years before she was born. As had become ritual, Addie continued to point up at the sky and say, "Dada's in heaven with God." But then she started to say something that didn't make sense to me.

"Dada's in heaven with God, and Grammy's there too."

Not surprisingly, I was more than a little freaked out by that and immediately called my mom to make sure she was okay, breathing easier as soon as she answered the phone.

Then, a few days later, Addie said the same thing at a family dinner. Nobody knew what to do or say. When she got home, Nicole called me.

"Do you think Addie's talking about Dad because she doesn't have a word for grandpa?" she wondered.

"I don't know."

So I took out my phone and showed Addie a picture of my father, which I had never done before.

"Who is this?" I asked her.

"That's Grammy!"

I zoomed out, because my mom was in the photo too, and said, "No, this is Grammy."

Then I pointed to my dad standing next to her. "Where's Grammy?"

And she pointed to my dad again.

Adalyn had never seen a picture of him before. So how could she know he was in heaven with Dada?

It made me think back to her playing peekaboo on the couch with someone other than me, made me wonder even more about the parts of our world we'll never understand because maybe we're not supposed to.

I first met Andy at Johnson Williams Middle School when we were both in seventh grade. He was the new kid, as they say, but he owned the place as soon as he set foot through the door. I remember the first time I saw him from the stands during gym class. I watched him laughing with everyone, fitting right in. And I was thinking something like, *Who does he think he is?* Not being all that socially confident, I was either jealous or offended—maybe both.

We talked about it later, and he explained how being a military brat led to him moving around a lot for his dad's postings. This was the tenth different town his family had lived in, so he had developed a talent for making friends since he had no idea how long he might be around them. I wouldn't call us friends until we reached high school, when he texted me for the first time. And the rest is pretty much history.

We enjoyed being together, no matter what we did. Andy played football and I ran cross country. We ran track together each spring, attended every high school dance, and just reveled in being high school kids in love.

I loved waiting for him after every football game. Except this one game his dad attended when he was home for a few weeks, and I remember Andy saying, "Don't wait for me after the game. My dad's here, and I don't know how it's going to go because of how I played."

He smiled and tailored his comment to sound light, even funny, but I could tell he was hurting inside. His dad was home through most of our senior year, but Andy wasn't. I'll never know all the ins and outs of what happened, but Andy ended up at his best friend Colton's house around three in the morning one night with a basket full of his clothes. He never returned home. Colton's family, the Chranes, became our family too. They held a very special place for Andy in their family and still do even in his death. There was no one better for the job of taking in Andy King than that family. After his death, I brought Addie out to Texas, where they live now, to meet them all. It was probably one of the most wholesome visits I've ever had. Sitting on the large porch every morning and evening telling Andy stories and catching up. They are a few of the people that knew Andy on as deep of a level as I did. Things all of us know, that the rest of the world would never be able to comprehend. I reunited with Colton and his siblings who were like siblings to Andy at one point as well. Colton has kids now too and we got to watch our kids play together, a moment I am sure Andy did not miss.

I can't help wondering about all those notes on his phone planning for Addie's future, what year she'd start this or that, and how that relates to the hardships Andy experienced as a child. He took his role as a dad so seriously because of his own home life growing up. It's amazing Andy emerged from that experience a loving person who gave so much of himself to others. That's such a testament to the kind of person he was and how lucky I was to have him in my life for as long as I did, with a wonderful little girl to show for it. We didn't get to finish our dream, but a lot of people never get as far as we did, even with all the time in the world.

The Call came at the most difficult time for any young couple's marriage, when we were new parents with our lives no longer centered on each other but on raising our daughter. We weren't the best versions of ourselves, and I mourn who Andy would've evolved and grown into even more than I mourn the Andy I lost.

On my first trip to South Carolina to visit Adam and Caylee, Andy's brother and his wife, after Andy's death, I remember verbalizing my regrets about our marriage to Caylee's mom Leslee over tea.

"Amy," she said, "everyone goes through that hard part of their marriage when they first have kids. Y'all just didn't get the time. A few more years and you would have figured it all out. You would have found your rhythm, and you guys would have been fine. The only thing y'all needed was time for your daughter to grow up a little so it would get a little easier and you don't always feel you're in the trenches."

Andy and I didn't have that time.

If only I could have truly saved time in a bottle, as the great Jim Croce song suggests. Since I can't, I have no choice but to be resilient and step up for Addie as well as myself. Not to take anything for granted and be present in every moment, because I've realized you never know what the next one will bring.

Losing Andy changed my view of life.

Losing Andy made me a better person.

Losing Andy made me see the world differently.

And one of my greatest regrets in all this is that the next person I meet will experience a more finished and healed version of myself than Andy ever got to see. The less controlling version, the less negative version. Andy missed out on getting to meet the carefree, live-in-the-moment version of me. I wish so badly that he could meet me where I am now. Andy was also the person who knew everything about me. With his death, so many stories and memories of me died with him. I miss hearing his renditions of our wedding day and the birth of Adalyn. No one will ever know me to the depths that he did. We grew up together and were both still growing when I got The Call. The thought of explaining the loss of Andy, not to mention my dad, to someone new one day feels overwhelming.

Speaking of which, when Addie's day care center/preschool celebrated National Grandparents Day, I was struck by the fact that almost all the kids had at least three and usually four grandparents; one kid, believe it or not, had *six*! And I remember thinking, *Dang, that's a lot!* With my dad's death and the estrangement of Andy's parents, Adalyn functionally only has one. But my sister-in-law, Caylee's parents have more than made up for that by becoming surrogate grandparents to her. She calls them Grammy Leslee and Grumps. At some point, I guess I will explain to Addie that we're not really related to them, but for now they're playing a vital role in her life. It's hard enough with all the other kids in her class having fathers. I don't want her to be the only one in school with a single grandparent, so I plan on enlisting them when the time comes.

There really isn't a book to consult on all of this, no set of rules to follow when it comes to dealing with grief, especially with a young child. Everyone has to go about it their own way. Do what's best for you. That may mean not following the advice of someone whose experience may have been entirely different from yours. We all have to chart our own courses back to happiness and fulfillment, because Google Maps can't get us there. We can plug in the starting point, but not the destination.

You know what scares me the most? The fact that as adults we can recall events starting only at between three and four years old, and that experiential memories really don't start taking hold until a child is between four and five. Well, Addie was only seventeen months when The Call came, so I wonder, without lasting memories of Andy, if he'll become a face in a picture or a figure in a family video, an image in her mind. She might keep hugging and kissing his photo, might always recognize his Helena hat, might never see an American flag without thinking of him, but she won't point to the image on my sweatshirt or hanging over the entrance to Lowe's and say "That's Dada's flag!" forever. Still, those things are all she has now, leaving them as the basis of her relationship with Andy. And I'm so grateful for that because they're still present in our everyday life, daily reminders, and I worry that without them he would slip away from her entirely.

Addie has so much of Andy in her. She is actually pretty good at sharing during playtime at day care. She doesn't mind giving up a toy after she has had it for a while; she just needs an explanation as to why. She wants the information and is a born negotiator. If you tell her she can have the toy back soon, she'll want to know how long, even though she can't tell time yet. And, like Andy, she's stubborn. They tell me she's the youngest kid in the whole class, but also the smartest, which reinforces my answer whenever someone asks me what I think she'll be when she grows up.

"A CEO!" I tell them unabashedly.

Most moms probably don't think about what their toddlers will take to school for show-and-tell once they reach kindergarten or first grade. I guess kids normally bring in their favorite toy, game, book, stuffed animal, maybe a souvenir from their trip to New York City or Disney World. In Addie's case, I know it will be one of the flags that will forever adorn her room, probably the one in the ceremonial glass-top case she was given at Andy's funeral service.

So while the other kids will be saying things like, "Mickey Mouse gave me this," or "I got to Level Ten on this game," or "This is the Empire State Building and I bought it at a store at the very top," Addie will hold up the case and say:

"This is my daddy's flag."

CHAPTER 7

Marital Status

"Are you married or single?"

So many things become run of the mill to the point that they don't warrant a first thought, much less a second. Like filling out medical forms when you go in for a checkup.

The first visit I made to my OB/GYN after The Call proved to be anything but that. It was the first time since Andy's passing that I was asked my marital status. The office was packed and there was a line behind me. Instead of giving me paperwork to fill out, the receptionist started asking me questions out loud quickly to put my information in the system. The office was now affiliated with a different hospital and had to redo the paperwork for their new booking system, leaving my marital status an unanswered question.

Most were routine: address, phone number, insurance carrier and number. The usual things, until we got to the one that froze me.

"What's your marital status?" she asked, in front of everyone in the waiting room.

I almost said single, but that didn't feel right, and they knew I was married before, so I said, "I'm widowed."

That word felt so dirty to say. I hate the word *widow*. I have been proud of every label society has placed on me: daughter, sister, mother, wife. But this one, I hate being associated with.

She did a double take, clearly embarrassed by having posed the question in the first place and not knowing how to respond.

"It's okay," I said, to take the pressure off her.

She nodded, looking relieved.

The waiting room was full, and the line behind me stretched almost to the door. Everyone stared, as if wondering if they'd heard right. How could that be, since I was one of the youngest women in the room? Andy and I had probably sat in every one of those chairs at some point, there for one of my many appointments when we were having Adalyn.

It was even hard driving there along the same route we had taken together to the office so many times, especially near the end of my pregnancy when some complications arose. Andy came with me to every single one, and we would stop at Chick-fil-A on the way home every time. It was like taking kids out for ice cream or pizza, win or lose, after a game. No matter how stressful the day turned out, we always had Chick-fil-A to look forward to.

I was spared further scrutiny when I was called back to the examination area to see my doctor and walked down the same hallway Andy and I walked down for regular ultrasounds, the same hallway we brought Addie down as a newborn. It felt like I was walking along the halls of someone else's life.

I entered the exam room and was met by another nurse with clipboard in hand, ready to fire off some more questions.

"Has anything about your health changed?" she asked me.

"No, not really. Well, I am on some medication now."

I updated her on what I was taking and she wrote down everything diligently. Then she regarded the form the nurse at the front had filled out, and I could see her tense a bit.

"You're not using any birth control?" she asked.

"No," I said.

"Then what are you using for contraceptives? Are you using condoms?"

"No."

She appeared to be miffed by that. "Well, are you planning a pregnancy then?"

I knew exactly what she was getting at and finally said, "My husband just died, so I'm not sexually active right now, and I don't have any plans to change that anytime soon."

I could see she was even more uncomfortable than the nurse behind the receptionist desk had been. She couldn't stop saying she was sorry.

"It's fine," I said, relieving the guilt yet another person was feeling. "Please stop apologizing. I'm fine."

I should have expected this. It's the reason I dread having new appointments anywhere I haven't been since The Call, because I never know when I'll have to address Andy's passing or whether I even should. My anxiety driving to this one and others was off the charts, because I'd become tired of absolving other people of their guilt for not knowing, and I still am. Normally, I try to avoid telling people. But then it inevitably gets to a point when I have to tell them, no matter where I am or who I'm talking to, and I'm tired of making others feel better about the situation when dredging it up with strangers makes me feel worse.

There was a time over Christmas break when I was with Andy's family in South Carolina and we took all the kids to a park to play. A mom there was playing with her little girl, who was a little older than Adalyn. The mom was so friendly and instantly struck up a conversation with me. We started talking about being new parents, the debate of day care versus staying at home with them, and all the usual topics. She asked why I was in town and I said I was visiting my husband's family. She proceeded to ask where I was from. Then she said that she was a stay-at-home mom and was very fortunate that her husband could work and provide for them. I told her I did the same for the first year of Adalyn's life. She asked me what my husband did for a living, and I remember I paused for a second. I couldn't tell this jovial mom at the park about what had just happened to my life. No one wants to hear that, especially a mom of a daughter Addie's age. So I lied. I talked about Andy like he was still alive.

The nurse left the exam room, the doctor came in, and it was the same thing all over again.

I didn't know. I'm so sorry. I just heard about Andy.

It always blew my mind that there were still people on this earth who didn't know Andy died, since I was living with that reality, consumed by it at that point. How could they not know when it seemed like everyone else did? And the conversations would always end the same way.

It's okay. I'm okay. It's all right.

But it wasn't.

On my way out of the exam room, I saw a family with their baby sitting just outside in the same chairs in the hallway that Andy and I had occupied countless times after ultrasounds of our baby girl. We would sit in those exact chairs with our little black-and-white photo and joke about who she looked like more. The couple was smiling and happy, bouncing their baby on their knees, their whole futures before them with no idea how fast life can change forever. You can't, until it happens to you. And I am no longer the same woman who used to come into that office anymore.

I've gotten to the point where I just come out and tell people flatly that "Andy died in a Humvee rollover" with a straight face. I've said it so many times, and the only time I ever cried after saying it was in my first visit to a therapist after receiving The Call. Prior to that, I vowed to be strong for everyone else, to keep going and be there for my child. As a result, I ended up getting really sick. My body was shutting down. I couldn't eat or sleep, and I was on different medications to cope with anxiety. I lost fifteen pounds I didn't have to lose. I was coughing and had a sore throat, even lost my voice before the funeral service and was worried I wouldn't be able to deliver the words I'd written from the podium. I went to an urgent care center to take a COVID test, and one of the questions they asked me was, "Who do you want to put down as your emergency contact?"

Which made me realize I didn't have an emergency contact anymore.

Nicole was sitting beside me and gave me the most defeated look ever. So I gave them her name and phone number.

Things like that are what hit the hardest, things we all take for granted and think nothing of, until our world is turned upside down and nothing is the same anymore.

Raising a toddler through all this made things difficult, but also more bearable. Difficult in the sense that I had to feed Addie, bond with her, take her to school, be present for her even when I was having trouble being present for myself. And it made things more bearable because she was the only light in the darkness of my life, giggling and doing the goofy things toddlers do where you can't help but smile. If it wasn't for Addie, I wouldn't have had any reason to get out of bed. She needed to wake up, have her eggs cooked, travel to school. At night we would paint, sharing wonderful moments of creating something together. Those were the only times I felt truly happy.

The impact wasn't just mental, though, it was also physical. I was still breastfeeding Addie once or twice a day when Andy died. Then, with all the stress and anxiety, I stopped cold turkey after The Call. Addie carried on like nothing changed, went right to drinking out of a sippy cup, while I suffered a huge shift in body chemistry. My hormones just crashed, which hit me even harder, because breastfeeding had been a very sacred thing for me. It was something I fought so hard for during the first four months of Adalyn's life. I didn't give it up even when it caused me agonizing pain for weeks, and I ended up going to multiple lactation consultants to get things figured out. I had been suffering from postpartum depression and was feeling like an unfit mother, because my body wasn't doing what it was supposed to. But I was adamant in my commitment to making this work. Having to stop cold turkey meant I had lost these magical moments between mother and daughter, making me feel like The Call robbed me of more than just Andy. It robbed me of *me*, and of experiences I could no longer enjoy alone as much as I had with him.

A part of my motherhood had been taken away, because I wasn't able to really enjoy this vital formative time in Adalyn's life. This cloud hung over me that darkened the more my health suffered and my stress levels refused to abate. We like to paint this picture of an idyllic motherhood. You see it in the movies, television, and social media on people's Facebook and Instagram feeds. But it's not that way for a lot of women, a reality my experience drove home in the wake of The Call.

Does that sound selfish? I don't mean it to. I had to find a way I could take care of myself so I could take care of my daughter. I'm only sharing the realities of what I was facing, what a lot of women face when getting divorced, sparring over custody, or raising a child with disabilities. We exude a brave front in public, make it appear we're doing just fine to strangers, while inside we feel ourselves coming apart.

When you become a single parent, and the other parent is no longer in the picture, so much anxiety about death can overwhelm you. I felt so much pressure to keep up with my health, to exercise, to not die. I was so panicked at times because I was all my daughter had left, and I could not bear the thought of leaving her. I knew I needed to try and heal these deep wounds and lift some of the heaviness to be there for her mentally and emotionally, not just physically, and be strong for her, which meant I had to be strong for myself. The truth is, I have no idea where I would be if I didn't have her. She saved me in ways that she will never understand, something I consider to be a blessing.

Having experienced the grief process five years before with my dad left me aware of which healthy coping mechanisms were most effective for me. I knew not to consume alcohol every night to numb my pain. I knew simple things like reading a book and lighting a candle worked. But there would be moments where nothing helped. I'd get in bed at night, close my eyes, and all I kept seeing was Andy in that Humvee and the accident. I couldn't stop wondering what his last thought might have been, something I'll never know, which didn't stop me from fixating on it.

I know there's a way to grieve in a healthy manner, just like I know it will get better. No one needs to preach that to me. I'd like to tell you that traditional therapy helped, but it really didn't. I've been to several different therapists. The ones I've seen have all the tools and therapy strategies, but none of them could relate very well to what I was going through, and all of them were shocked by the level of self-awareness I was displaying. And it wasn't really grief I was suffering from so much as the lingering trauma from The Call itself informing me Andy had been in an accident.

I found some relief from a therapy called EMDR, or Eye Movement Desensitization and Reprocessing, which for me involved holding pulsators while I processed and talked about traumatic memories, the goal being to help desensitize the trauma in your mind. There are varying theories on its relative effectiveness, but I know it worked for me. EMDR may sound like a new form of treatment, but it's actually been around since the 1980s to treat post-traumatic stress disorder. Trauma can overwhelm the way the mind processes information, leaving the memory stuck as though the experience is still happening, which prevents those suffering from moving past it. When people have PTSD, rather than remembering the trauma, recognizing it as disturbing, but knowing that it's over, they can feel as if they're reliving it. EMDR therapists utilize something called "bilateral dual attention stimulation," like side-to-side eye movements or pulsators, to help change the way memories are stored in order to move past the trauma.

For me, the treatment involved focusing on the accident while simultaneously holding those pulsators in each hand. Theoretically, the pulsators stimulate the brain to treat the traumatic memories like regular ones. Eventually, the distress associated with the memory in question dissolves. The sessions lasted only fifteen minutes but were exhausting. I was so tired after each one, I felt like I'd run a marathon. I had to go home and sleep, because my brain was spent.

I also joined a grief group with my pastor for six weeks, and that proved more effective than a lot of other therapies. Diving deeper into my faith was a huge part of my moving forward. My faith was the one constant I could reply upon.

There are so many ways we can help ourselves get past the worst times of our lives. We should never blame ourselves when one doesn't work. Everyone's different, and the key is to find what works for you, what makes you feel better and helps you move past your own trauma.

But there are some parts of trauma that are more difficult to overcome than others.

CHAPTER 8

Milestones

For me, that was, and continues to be, milestones, those times that form the benchmarks and mile markers of our lives. The good news is that Andy and I had been together so long, we were able to celebrate many of these moments together. The bad news is that there will be no more for us to share.

We got our driver's licenses together.

We graduated high school together.

We were each other's first true loves.

We went to Virginia Tech together.

We turned twenty-one together and went to our first NFL game together.

We rented our first apartment together, and I have a photo of the two of us holding up the lease. Andy was in uniform because he was still at Virginia Tech as a member of the Corps of Cadets. I graduated a year early, while he stayed to finish his final year.

We opened our first bank account together and bought our first house in Elkton when we were only twenty-two, just after we got married.

We also got our first dog together and, of course, had a wonderful daughter together. Interestingly, she was always Adalyn while Andy was alive. She only became Addie after The Call, which was one of the first milestones Andy missed.

And remember my Ford Expedition Max? It was the first brand-new car either of us had ever bought, and we did that together too.

We experienced so many things so young that I feel like we lived a full life together, even though it didn't last nearly long enough. We were always the first in our friend group to do pretty much everything. Get married, buy a house, have a baby, buy a second house—the list goes on and it's long.

But I'm also reminded of other milestones Andy never got to celebrate. A few chapters back, I wrote about how we put an offer in on a farm and that the financing was approved before Andy left for training. He enjoyed working for Helena so much in large part because it brought him into the world of farming that he loved to the point where his dream was to experience it from the other side as a farm owner. Although it wasn't written in the Notes app on his iPhone, Andy wanted to be a full-time farmer. The year before he died, he actually rented twenty acres from someone who planned to build a house on that land in the future. Twenty acres is tiny compared to the farms Andy serviced, but it was his, and he filled those acres with stalks of corn. Even though he didn't have the time to work a full-time farm of his own yet, he loved to ride in combines any chance he could.

Farming was his true passion. Andy's plan was to work for Helena into his early fifties and then become a customer of his successor. The farm we were on the verge of buying was a bridge to that dream, one of the many he never saw fulfilled. We both had so much to look forward to, and Andy would have needed forty hours in every day to get it all done. He was so driven that his days really did seem to last that long. He was forever wheeling and dealing, always with a plan in mind, until the one thing he couldn't possibly plan for happened.

I feel guilty about a lot of things: fights we had, words we've spoken to each other in the heat of a moment, the small stuff I didn't let go of, resentment toward him when becoming a mom, words left unsaid, and a goodbye I won't ever get. But the biggest of them all is perhaps that Andy had such a clear plan for his life and was so confident in the moves he made every day to get there even since college, and I on the other hand feel clueless about it a lot of days. I feel guilty that Andy knew exactly what he wanted to do and can't do it. He was completely robbed of that. I feel guilty for being here over him, and I try every day not to waste it. I try to live out his dreams some days and hop in a combine with one of his farmers, and I try to build the life for Adalyn that he would want her to have. And it absolutely kills me some days when I must let go of some of the things we had planned together.

But that's just it—it's not us "together" anymore, it's just me, so plans can't stay the same. You can honor the person and the dreams you had together as much as you can, but at the end of the day, most of those plans must be redrawn. Yes, I would have loved to farm with Andy and raise Addie that way we planned, but can I do that alone without sacrificing a lot of my time as a mom and my own goals? No, I can't. People always say, "This is what Andy would want," and sometimes that may be true, but if it's not…that's okay too.

Just about everybody who knew him would say Andy was fearless, except for one fear only I witnessed—specifically the fear of not being enough. He wanted to be the absolute best he could be at absolutely everything he did. I don't know if he was haunted by the fear of falling short, but he did all he could to make sure that never happened.

I believe in my heart that what drove Andy, to a great extent, was that his parents were absent for so many of the milestones of his life. They missed his high school graduation, his college graduation, his Army commissioning ceremony, his graduating from Airborne School at Fort Benning in Georgia. On that note, Andy was deathly afraid of heights. The only thing that scared him more was not being good enough, which drove him to allay his fear and jump out of airplanes ten thousand feet in the air. He used the fact that he was never good enough for his parents as motivation for always being good enough for himself.

Some people are terrified they'll make the same mistakes as their parents. Not Andy. He knew he would be a great dad, supremely confident about that in the same way he was about anything.

There was this time we were in the car together when he answered a call from his boss at Helena over the speaker.

"What's up? I'm in the car with Amy. You're on speaker. Say hi."

"Take me off speakerphone right now."

I could hear the anger in his boss's voice. Even when we were off speaker, I still heard it because he was yelling, chewing Andy out for doing something without asking again. And he would just take it. No regrets about the lines he would cross for his farmers.

Andy was never afraid to ask for forgiveness over permission. There were numerous times with his job when he pushed the limits and boundaries. But all of it was truly out of compassion for his farmers. If something needed to be done, he got it done. If a promise was made, he followed it through. No matter the trouble. He knew the phone call would come later, and his response was always the same: "I had to do it." He would always make it right later, but he would drive most people crazy in the process. But I like to think that was the part they loved and hated about Andy at the same time.

Andy was a "get it done" kind of guy. He didn't look at that as going out on a limb; he viewed it as the best way to climb a tree. Yes, he could be a pain at times, but that was because he was so damn good at what he was doing. He wanted to be the best husband, the best dad, the best friend, the best customer rep, the best soldier. Everyone loved him for the same reasons they wanted to hate him: They loved everything Andy did and his intentions behind it, but sometimes hated the way he did it.

In his eulogy, Lieutenant Colonel Hall told a story about the platoon he commanded spending a month in California training in practical war games that stressed preparation and readiness. Andy was company commander and out on a run when the other company launched an attack. Andy got word on his walkie-talkie and came barreling down the hill at full speed in his Physical Training uniform. Not bothering to change, he threw his vest and gear over his PT shorts and shirt and said, "It's go time!" At the end of the exercise, Hall related how everyone was standing in their full Army uniforms except Andy, who had his PT stuff on underneath. Hall took a picture of him and Andy said, "Hey, can I get that photo?" His reaction to standing out among the rest of the company when he saw it was, "That's sick."

I think that's what drove Andy's dream of becoming a full-time farmer while he was still young enough to enjoy it. He could be his own boss that way, no one to tell him how to do this or that.

Among the hardest things for me to deal with through the initial days, weeks, and even months was the disbelief friends, colleagues, and acquaintances expressed upon hearing the news.

His brother Adam was the first one I called, and our conversation kind of typified the responses of anyone who knew Andy. I told him about the awful feeling I had after being informed first about the accident, before I'd even gotten The Call.

"He'll be fine," Adam insisted.

"I don't think so," I said, "not this time."

"This is Andy we're talking about."

Andy might not have been immortal, but everyone who knew him considered him to be invincible. He was so positive, someone whose motor never stopped.

It doesn't sound good, I told other family members and friends in the time between those two calls. *I have a sick feeling that he isn't going to make it.*

What do you mean? came their collective response. *Like, he probably just needs surgery, right? This is Andy King. He's so strong and healthy, he can pull through anything. He's not going to die.*

That's the reason why people were so shocked when he did. That's what shook everyone, along with the suddenness of it all. Each time I made one of those calls, I relived the shock of the experience all over again. It wasn't good for me, but I didn't have a choice. There were people out there who deserved to hear the news from me specifically. I was still calling people at ten, eleven o'clock that night of The Call, pulling names and contact information from the computer because I didn't have Andy's phone back yet.

"Hey," I said to a friend of his at the outset of one of the last calls I placed, "have you heard about Andy today?"

"No, is he alright? Was I supposed to call him?"

"Has anyone called you about him?"

"No. What's going on, Amy?"

"Andy's not all right. There was an accident today and he didn't make it."

"What do you mean, he didn't make it?"

"He died."

It was almost like Andy's friend was mad at me for breaking the news to him, and his reaction was more or less typical. Nobody wanted to believe it, nobody *could* believe it, because this was Andy King.

Months later, I called our tree guy to have two trees removed from our yard.

"I'm Amy King," I greeted. "I live in Woodstock. You've removed some trees for us before."

"Sure. That's right. Your husband's in the army. How's he doing?"

"I'm sorry to have to tell you this, but Andy actually passed away."

"What?"

"There was an accident."

"Wow, I don't know what to say. You really stirred up my day here."

I almost told him I knew that feeling all too well.

I needed to adapt to living with only memories, one of my favorites being how Andy proposed to me. Virginia Tech traditionally hosted an annual Ring Dance for juniors and seniors held in the Squires Commonwealth Banquet Hall. The dance began with the Corps of Cadets, before expanding to include everyone, and dates all the way back to 1934. It's called the Ring Dance because it's where juniors receive their class rings, but there's also a tradition where a member of the Corps of Cadets proposes to his girlfriend. Well, little did I know that's what Andy had in store for me our junior year, since I would be graduating early.

All the cadets like Andy wear their dress uniforms. I was wearing a navy ball gown, and at dinner with friends prior to the dance, the waitress spilled a whole bowl of salad dressing all over it. I took things in stride, but Andy was going crazy, trying to swab it clean with club soda so there'd be no stain. He was wigging out, something he never did. I had told him I wanted to get engaged any time after I graduated a month later, but Andy had other plans. As the class ring ceremony got underway, he got down on one knee in front of everyone.

"Amy, I love you so much. I want to spend the rest of my life with you. Will you marry me?" he asked, holding the ring box open.

The cheers and applause were so loud, I don't think anyone even heard me say, "Yes!"

We both felt so happy and grateful with where our life was headed in that moment.

CHAPTER 9

Safe Haven

I have two tattoos, one on each forearm. The one on the left, in my father's handwriting, says *I miss you. Love, Dad.* The one on my right, in Andy's handwriting, reads *I love you,* followed by A^3 inside a heart. The significance of that is everyone used to call Andy and me "A-squared," and when Adalyn came along, we became "A-cubed."

Andy's last Facebook post came the day before the accident, steeped in irony since he shared our sister-in-law's post about our twin toddler nephews. He called himself, "A proud uncle of two very literal miracle babies and extremely proud of my brother and his wife for keeping faith through the journey."

Charlie and Henry were indeed miracle babies because they'd been born very premature, after only twenty-five weeks. We didn't know if they would make it, and they ended up spending a full five months in the neonatal ICU. Andy's brother Adam and his wife Caylee became an active ambassador family for the March of Dimes organization, the irony lying in the fact that a week after Andy's funeral, they were scheduled to speak at the

March of Dimes' annual fundraising gala event as the Family of the Year. Call it one of the cruel twists of life, made even more poignant by the fact Andy had only recently grown close again to Adam. I can't imagine what it must have felt like for them to be so happy that their miracle babies lived against all odds and having it be a night to celebrate, while in contrast to that, Andy had died in a matter of an instant just a few weeks prior despite being perfectly healthy.

Adam and Caylee have been hesitant to think about having more children because of the complicated labor. Caylee and I relate a lot on wanting more kids and knowing we can't expand our families the way we had originally hoped. I will never be able to give Adalyn a full-blood brother or sister. If she has siblings one day, they won't share the same dad. But Charlie, Henry, and Adalyn will grow up together, making them the closest thing to siblings.

I texted Andy that evening before the accident because he left for drill the night before.

`Have you seen the video your brother posted?`

This was a big deal because representatives from the March of Dimes came to Adam and Caylee's home and did an interview for a story about how the twins survived as part of their being named Family of the Year. Andy went to the link I texted him and reposted it.

Andy's post that he was proud of his brother meant so much to Adam because it ran counter to his family's utter dysfunction. So, for Andy to say he was proud of his brother meant far more than it would have for virtually anyone else. And it was the birth of the twins that spurred Andy to reconnect with Adam, after years of giving in to the whims of their parents who had created such a toxic family dynamic, in my opinion.

He extended an olive branch to Adam, thanks to a Helena supplier who got him tickets to the football game between the South Carolina Gamecocks (Andy and Adam's favorite college team) and the University of North Carolina at Bank of America Stadium in Charlotte, where the Carolina Panthers play their home games, by inviting his brother to join him. It worked out perfectly, because Adam and Caylee live only twenty minutes from Charlotte, just across the South Carolina border. I don't remember Andy ever telling me who won the game; I don't think he cared, being too busy rekindling his relationship with Adam in a kind of repudiation of the way they'd been parented. Another irony, given that they had become parents so close in time to each other. I do remember FaceTiming the twins on their second birthday the month before Andy passed. Strange how both he and Adam having children had forged the bond that brought them back together, overcoming their upbringing.

Adalyn was born less than a year after the twins, which made their newly forged bond even stronger. Believe it or not, she was the first little girl in a family that included only boys. And because the twins have an October birthday, the three kids will actually be entering kindergarten together.

The March of Dimes event Adam and Caylee were scheduled to speak at as Family of the Year was held only a week after Andy's funeral. It was such an emotional night for them. They should have been celebrating, but instead they were grieving.

"We're happy that our boys lived," Caylee told me later, fighting back tears, "but Andy just died and he was so healthy. It is a miracle the boys are alive, and there's a million reasons why Andy should be alive too."

Their miracle twins overcame all odds to survive their premature birth healthy and normal. That left me wondering what the odds were of Andy not being here to celebrate that March of Dimes gala with them.

For me, Adam and Caylee were a miracle themselves. Three weeks after the funeral, I couldn't bear the thought of having Thanksgiving in Woodstock with Andy gone and was so happy when they invited Adalyn and me to Fort Mill to join them for the holiday. They live in this nice cookie-cutter neighborhood where all the homes look exactly the same, right down to the size of the backyards, so different from the rural farm community of Woodstock. There are tons of grocery stores, and all the land is developed with commercial buildings, office parks, strip malls, and shopping plazas instead of rolling open space. And I embraced that maybe because I felt so much emptiness inside that I welcomed the busyness outside and found it refreshing.

I was still such a mess that week I couldn't even drive myself down there. My mom had to drive Adalyn and me to a Cracker Barrel off Route 81 situated at almost exactly the halfway point between my house and theirs in Fort Mill. Caylee pulled in just after us, we switched Addie's car seat to her car, and off we went.

The whole way to Fort Mill, Caylee and I did not stop talking, just debriefing from everything that had happened earlier that month, a few weeks that felt like a lifetime. We hadn't seen each other since the funeral, and we cried and talked about how Adam really wanted to be there for Adalyn in any capacity he could. He just wanted to do right by Andy, perhaps in part to make up for the years they lost. It was such an emotional conversation, because none of us had been really close before the accident. We were getting there, and Andy's death served to jump-start the process.

I posted this on Facebook Thanksgiving morning:

> "Say not in grief 'he is no more' but live in thankfulness that he was."
>
> I did not know that every first holiday as a family would also be our last. Today feels so wrong without you and always will. We will never move on but we will try to move forward.
>
> Even in loss, I am so thankful for each and every person who has reached out through messages, comments, phone calls, and mail. I may not respond, but they are carrying me through this. I am eternally grateful for what all of you have done for me these last few weeks. Thank you.

I actually stayed with Caylee's parents, Addie's aforementioned surrogate Grammy and Grumps, because Andy and I had never stayed there before, meaning there were no memories. The Antilleys live in a beautiful house with a pool on a few acres. Every time we go there now, Addie gets to swim and smile and laugh, making this and Caylee's home my little slice of South Carolina heaven, my safe haven. Like Andy and Adam, she and I were starting to get close before, but we became like best friends, sisters really. We talk every day instead of, maybe, twice a year. Over Thanksgiving weekend, we had a really deep conversation about what we wanted our roles to be going forward, what we wanted this family to look like. And we were all pretty much on the same page of wanting and needing to build Adalyn her village and being there for each other. No more excuses for how she and Adam didn't have time to come to Virginia, or I didn't have time to go to South Carolina.

The fact that she might not be able to have any more children deeply saddened Caylee because, like me, she always dreamed of having a big family. Even though hers hasn't gotten any smaller the way mine has, both of our families have gotten bigger because of our friendship. Addie and the twins are more like siblings than cousins. They steal each other's toys and give each other these little hugs that warm my heart and helped restore my sense of hope.

At the end of that Thanksgiving weekend, Caylee brought Adalyn and me back to the same Cracker Barrel parking lot, where my mother picked us up. For Christmas, I drove back by myself. Even though my friends and neighbors had rallied around me, I didn't want to be home for that holiday without Andy.

I posted this on Facebook Christmas morning:

> I was able to spend the last week surrounded by Andy's family, where I feel him the most. Christmas was hands down his favorite holiday. I realize now how magical and special he made it for me now that it's all gone. It's days like today that feel like I'm being told he's not coming home all over again. These days make reality hit. A day you can't ignore the absence of someone. I have been with Andy since my freshman year of high school. Without a doubt I remember more holidays with him than without.
>
> Yet it's still amazing to me how so much joy can exist in so much grief. I have spent many painful

> moments alone and in tears this week and then minutes later in complete joy and laughter. Watching Adalyn grow and get to know her extended family and friends has been the biggest blessing over the holidays this year. She makes everything lighter and has no idea how much she is carrying me through grief. I will always continue to move forward for her and try to be the fun parent now and live in the moment like Andy, so she can experience what I did having him in my life.
>
> "But those who hope in the Lord will renew their strength. They will soar on wings like eagles; they will run and not grow weary, they will walk and not be faint." Isaiah 40:31 (NIV)

For me in my new normal, social media has become an outlet to vent, as well as offer thanks to those who've been there for me ever since The Call. Interestingly enough, Addie and I have gotten very close with other members of Andy's family too, just not his parents. His Uncle Wayne, brother to Andy's estranged mother, has become more a part of our lives too. In fact, he was one of those who received a flag at Andy's funeral service. And every time we drive to Fort Mill, we make a stop in Columbia, South Carolina, to visit Wayne and his family, as well as Andy's grandparents on his mom's side.

They couldn't make the funeral because they can't travel, so the first time we made the trip, we met them at Chick-fil-A for lunch. After lunch, I gave Andy's grandma a hug. She hugged me back and started sobbing.

"Please don't forget about us," she implored, in between the tears.

It hit me then that with Andy gone, they were worried Addie and I would disappear from their lives. As things turned out, though, we see them more now than we ever did before The Call. Andy's other brother Alex is in the navy, stationed in Canada. So Adam, Caylee, and I went to visit him and his wife Lauren there.

"I want you to be happy, but, selfishly, I don't want you to ever meet someone else, because I'm scared we won't see you and Adalyn anymore," Alex confided in me. "I'm scared you won't make the effort anymore."

We're all he has left of Andy, and he's scared of losing that.

"That won't happen," I tried to reassure him. "You guys have to trust me."

I think it's hard for Adam and Alex to do that because of the way they were raised. But I meant what I said, because nothing's more important to me than keeping Andy's presence alive, and that starts with his family.

I follow a lot of fellow widows' pages on Facebook, and their posts serve as a cautionary tale. So many posts I see are about how they don't speak to their deceased spouse's family anymore. That things went south at some point, and they've moved on. Too often, the relationship soured over money, who got what when their husband died, or people got upset that they were dating again. I never wanted it to be that way with Andy's family. Adam and Caylee didn't even expect to be around the week leading up to the funeral, and having them all there opened a door I don't intend to close. And every time I read one of those widows' posts on Facebook to the contrary, I feel so grateful to have them in my life. Most people will judge you in every decision you make in your life, especially as a twenty-seven-year-old widow who is under a microscope, and I am so grateful I have never felt judged by Andy's brothers. They have grown to trust my decisions for myself and their little niece, and they support me endlessly.

Too often, it seems, I see other posts that bemoan the fact that nobody comes around anymore, and how the support wears off. In my opinion, as the griever, you have to make the effort to ask for the support and let the people in your life know what you need. Many people have not experienced something like this, and I guarantee they are thinking about you constantly, but they have no idea what to do. You have to forge your own safe haven, not wait for someone else to do it for you. But if you are reading this as a friend or family member of a griever, I have only one piece of advice to you: Just show up.

Andy was almost always extremely frugal…until it came to Christmas, where he operated with an unlimited budget. Our first Christmas without him arrived around six weeks after The Call and was really hard on me.

Andy was adamant about having a real tree every year. I had a real tree growing up and he never did, so I was kind of done with them because they're so darn messy, especially with three dogs running around.

"Let's get a fake tree," I'd suggest every year.

"Nope," Andy would say, "we have to get a real tree. Because I never had a real tree growing up. I want a real tree. I want my house to smell like a Christmas tree."

Of course, I gave in, and now I will be getting a real tree forever.

Understandably, I wasn't in the mood that December. So two of the Six Friends insisted on taking me to pick one out. Wait, it gets better. It turns out the Woodstock Auxiliary Fire

Department sponsors a family each year and decorates their home. Andy had told me that this year we were going big, that we were going to have every square inch of the house decorated in lights and all the trimmings. I wasn't of a mind to manage that either, so the Woodstock Auxiliary Fire Department showed up while I was out with friends getting our Christmas tree.

Well, I came home to find Christmas lights strung along the front of the house and across the roof, lighting up the reindeer and blow-up Santa adorning my front yard. Everything was aglow, the way Andy would have wanted. We came in, put the tree up, and it was like a scene from a Hallmark movie, as we decorated the boughs with lights. And that wasn't all. We were stringing the lights while eating a bunch of food all our friends and family had brought along, when Santa himself came strolling up the driveway. All the kids ran straight to him. I can't tell you how much it meant to me that all these people had gone so far out of their way to create such a wonderful memory for Addie and me. To think that The Call had come just over a month before. I wondered if I'd ever smile again and, on this night, I couldn't stop. The Christmas spirit might not be a cure for all ills, but I know I'll remember Christmas of 2023 fondly for the rest of my life.

Which wasn't where I was on New Year's Eve. This particular milestone has always been hard for me since my dad passed, harder even than Thanksgiving or Christmas, because in this case, it marked the end of the last year Andy and I were together. And 2024 was a year he could never see or know about. I remember thinking the same thing when my dad died. It was so disconcerting to enter a year you know a loved one will never get to experience. It was just this weird feeling that Andy wouldn't be around to witness history anymore. My friends saved the day by planning a small "celebration" with me that included my sister Nicole and brother-in-law Trae, but that only went so far, and I cried the loudest I had yet when the calendar turned to a new year without Andy. We didn't even do the countdown thing, but it didn't matter. Everyone knew it was midnight, and my sister and friends greeted 2024 crying with me, all of us holding each other.

Milestones aren't reserved for holidays, though, and it reached the point where so many everyday things with Addie left me thinking of how much Andy was missing. Like when we went to our annual local fair, the same fairgrounds where Andy's funeral was held, and she rode her first kiddie ride, grinning from ear to ear inside a plastic whale. And I was thinking, *Andy would have freaking loved this....* And she doesn't sleep with her foxy anymore, she sleeps with Mr. Cow. All the clothes he last saw her in don't fit her, and she sleeps in two-piece pajamas now instead of her onesies. Her little ponytail is now a big ponytail that can hold all her hair.

There are so many things like that, small things that keep popping up. Andy and I used to have coffee together out of this big pot I'd make every morning. Now I've switched to individual K-cups, and I hate it. I miss my pot of coffee, because it reminds me of how much I miss Andy. We're a family of two now, not three, and that means when I'm not with Addie, I'm alone. Little things like K-cups remind you you're by yourself.

CHAPTER 10

Dark Winter

The ensuing months made up my darkest period, riddled with times I thought I was never going to feel any better, that I'd be grieving and lost forever. I think of them as my dark winter, even though they spilled into spring and even summer. The sun warmed up and the flowers bloomed, but I still felt cold and colorless inside.

My dark winter started when we left for the Bahamas shortly after New Year's Day. One of the last things Andy and I did together was take Addie to get her passport, since this would be her first time leaving the country, and being on an airplane, for that matter. Both parents have to be present to get a child's passport, so we got her little photo taken and a month later her passport arrived in the mail.

We'd made all the arrangements back in August, the last event we planned together. That would have made the trip hard on its own, but it wasn't going to be just immediate family. It was kind of an extended family reunion.

I tried to leave multiple times, tried to get a flight back home. But we were on a tiny island at the edge of the Bahamas where the airport boasted little service, and it was impossible to book seats. When you're grieving, the last thing you need is to be stuck on an island with everyone celebrating a vacation after you just endured the most gut-wrenching experience of your life. I was still barely eating a full meal at this point and still fifteen pounds underweight. Grief can make you cranky and short with people, snapping at them for pushing your buttons. They don't know what to say, so they end up saying all the wrong things.

Normally that wouldn't bother me, but being so far away from home, outside of my comfort zone, I hyper-focused on every misplaced word or comment, no matter how well intentioned. There was nothing else there for me to focus on. It was a rowdy group, celebrating each other's company, when the last thing I wanted to do was celebrate anything at all. And because of the unfamiliar surroundings, every little thing set me off, stuff that I would otherwise take in stride even in my new normal. If people joked with me or got on me too hard, I would end up bawling my eyes out. I felt so fragile. Like my heart was made of glass and any small bump in the day or misplaced memory could just crack it wide open. It still feels like that some days. I could only compartmentalize my grief for such small moments in time.

But the worse thing is when people don't say anything at all, because maybe they are afraid of saying the wrong thing, but it is such an isolating feeling when people can't acknowledge the absence in the room when it is so glaring to you. I don't hold a grudge about these things because to be honest, even now when I hear about someone passing, I don't know how to act or what to say either. I get it. The hard thing to do is to acknowledge the undeniable reality, but I think it is the right thing to do. I promise we are already thinking of this person every minute of every day, and you acknowledging it isn't bringing it to surface, because it's already indelibly present there.

This trip overall was the one time in the grieving process when I failed to follow my instincts. I never should have gone on the trip. I didn't want to be there. And as soon as I got there, all I wanted to do was take Addie home. Despite seeing the trip as a setback to my emotional recovery, I also saw Addie do a whole bunch of things that made me smile. She swam fearlessly with sea turtles and stingrays, and even petted them. Those were heightened moments of joy for me that only exacerbated how hard it was to be around everyone else, trying to make them happy because I didn't want to be Debbie Downer. That trip was probably so magical for Adalyn, having her grammy, auntie, and Uncle Trae with her on a beautiful island with all her favorite sea animals. I look back at the photos now, and I just see so much pain behind every smiling photo I'm in. I can feel the emptiness in me when I see those photos. Like my body is standing there but nobody is inside.

Getting back home was such a relief, and I splurged a bit on my birthday a couple weeks later in January. I rented out an Airbnb, this beautiful old home in Charlottesville, Virginia, near the campus of UVA. Andy always went all out on my birthday, and the weekend brought back happy memories of the last one we shared together. We stayed at the George Washington Hotel in Winchester, and he hired a car for the night to take us out to dinner in Leesburg and then back to where we were staying. He was a master of surprising me with the best gifts. Reflecting on that made me think of how much we differed on some things, like events. Andy was all about the macro, while I was always more focused on the micro. But for this birthday I adopted his attitude. It was just my closest friends, along with Caylee, and my sister Nicole. We ate great food, toured the nearby wine country, and I actually enjoyed myself. And yet there were moments when I couldn't help but fixate on the fact I had no one to check in with, to text or email about the great time I was having, or just to say I miss you. In my dark winter, a heaviness pervaded every event; no matter how much I wanted the sun to shine down on me, there was always a cloud.

Speaking of which, letting some light in that weekend only made the darkness feel even deeper. I knew I needed a plan, needed something to look forward to, because it would make me feel less guilty for languishing in bed the rest of my time. I began staying at my sister's house a lot, weekends and some weeknights, and that was so helpful to my healing, providing respite by simply getting out of my own house. She also lived closer to my mom, and that allowed me to see her more and get tremendous help with my dogs and Addie. I had three dogs and a toddler that my mom has helped me coparent ever since The Call.

The saying "no matter how old you get, you always need your mom" holds true. Not many mothers and daughters share the unique experience of being widows together at such young ages. She watched me lose my dad and I watched her lose her husband. And now she was watching me lose my husband and I was watching Addie lose her dad. With Andy's sudden death and my dad's death being a suicide, we both had so much trauma from those experiences. We don't know the slow and peaceful death. Only the fast kind with no goodbyes. And even though she lost my dad five years prior, I could tell she was at a loss about how to help me sometimes, because it was just so unfathomable.

My family has been through so much, but on the other side, it has emerged a healthy and loving family who does not take for granted the life we get to live. I think all of us are so permanently changed by this. We have way fewer trivial arguments. We don't let disagreements fester. We take the trips. We take the time to love on each other and be there for each other in the small day-to-day phone calls and on the big vacations as well. We show up for each other. We root for each other. I am proud of us because each and every one of us crawled our ways out of the deepest holes to mourn my dad and Andy—our father, brother, son, and husband. And we get to live our lives with this unique perspective on what really matters, like Addie will too.

At Nicole's house, my brother-in-law Trae would take Addie on little tractor rides around the yard. They would entertain her while I cooked dinner to contribute. I always tried to have a plan centered around never being at my own home more than two days a week to avoid the familiar triggers. The house had become stifling for me, full of memories and experiences that kept me in my pain. For two months, there'd been so many things to plan for the holidays and so many arrangements to make after The Call. Now, there was nothing left to plan, no task to focus on. It felt like I had dropped into a void.

When I was home, after dropping Addie off at day care, I'd end up lying in bed all day watching Netflix. My primary coping mechanisms became bingeing shows and scrolling through my phone. Believe it or not, the saddest and most emotional movies were the ones I gravitated to the most as a way, I guess, of not shying away from what I was feeling. And, since I had a plan, since I was already looking forward to my next sleepover, I was able to grin and bear that.

Being at home brought a numbness with it, almost as if my emotions were scarred over. I was convinced then, and am even more convinced today, that the worst recipe to healing emotionally is to live 100 percent in the situation you are in. Anything you can do to create a different environment for yourself, short of bingeing bars instead of television shows, is a big net positive. If I hadn't stayed with my sister or Caylee so often, I would have spent that entire dark winter lying in bed, rotting and sulking. I think back now to what my healing actually looked like and realize much of it happened on the fly, based on my emotional impulse and having the courage to admit I wasn't strong enough to stand on my own. Instead, I learned to let myself be pulled along on the coattails of others until I was ready to pick myself back up.

I definitely wasn't there yet on Andy's March 25 birthday. I was with Adam and Caylee down in South Carolina, and I pretty much cried all day. There was no hiding behind festivities for a holiday that everyone was celebrating, no distraction from the harsh reality that this was Andy's day and only Andy's day. I could disassociate a bit, or make myself be strong for Addie, on the more communal holidays. But that wasn't the case here. We bought a little cake, lit a single candle, and sang "Happy Birthday," after which Addie blew out the candle. The strangest thing about that day was when we FaceTimed with Andy's other brother Alex, who happened to be wearing a hat for the occasion. Addie looked at him, smiled broadly, and said, "Dada!" I honestly believe she thought it was Andy on the other end of the line, calling in from heaven.

I went back to South Carolina again for Easter, which we celebrated at Caylee's mom's house. We did an Easter egg hunt for Addie and the twins, and it was hilarious because Caylee's mom stuffed the eggs full of too many snacks. Do you have any idea how long it takes a toddler to eat five Goldfish? Every time they found an egg, this trio of toddlers would plop themselves down and start munching. Needless to say, the parents did a lot of the hunting.

Easter made me think about church, where I'd basically stopped going, except for Pastor Nate's incredible Bible study classes that focused on grief. Until that year, I loved Easter because it was all about rejoicing and celebrating without all the preparation. It had always been my favorite holiday, but it had become the hardest one for me.

I finally went back to church without Andy for the first time around Mother's Day and sat down in the same pew by myself where we'd always sat together. A bunch of my friends were all sitting directly in front of me and came closer to join me. I didn't think it was going to be a particularly emotional experience, and it wasn't until I took communion, at which point the tears burst out of me. I felt Andy's loss so deeply in that moment. Communion speaks of life, death, and resurrection. It made me confront my loss directly. To really think about where Andy was because of what Jesus did for us. Hearing the words "do this for the remembrance of me" suddenly had a different meaning inside me. Secondly, there may not be a time since before high school when, if I was taking communion, Andy wasn't by my side. I never went to church without him there. His absence in that moment was palpable. The ritual felt incomplete.

Communion also invited a vulnerability inside me. It was like I knew God had been with me this entire time, but I kept Him at a distance. Like "I know you're here, God, but I am mad at you and need space, but I want to talk about it later." And in that moment, I felt like I was confronting Him for the first time. It was never that I didn't believe in Him; I just couldn't face Him.

Sometimes people would ask me if I'd lost my faith and felt let down by God. I would always tell them no; that said, I was really struggling with prayer.

Why am I praying? What am I praying for? If this is already written out, why does it matter?

I spoke with Pastor Nate about this. I felt like I had prayed to God so many times for the safety and health of my family and it didn't happen. So why pray? And Nate said to me, "God promises faith, not fairness."

I began saying that to myself every day, often multiple times, and it has become a vital part of my healing process. I have since learned that prayer is about connection, comfort, gratitude, and surrender.

"When you ask for something you want really, really bad," Pastor Nate told me, "God has three answers: yes, no, and not right now. And sometimes the not right now answer is the hardest to deal with."

Even though I began to feel better after my return to church, *not quite yet* best described my lengthening dark winter, because Memorial Day held the darkest moment of all. I spent the long weekend back in South Carolina with Adam, Caylee, and Caylee's family. I didn't expect it to be hard, but then it hit me that Andy was associated with this day now. It hadn't registered with me up until that point, and I woke up the next morning feeling this pressing anxiety. I had always celebrated Memorial Day as gratitude for our fallen service members, but it is so much deeper and complex for me now. I remember walking into Caylee's mom's house for the family cookout and just started bawling my eyes out.

I couldn't get past the fact that Memorial Day was like a party holiday in the minds of everyone. And I'm sure many of those service members in heaven would probably prefer it to be just that, not sad, like I'm sure Andy would too. But in my mind this first year, the final Monday in May should have been treated as a more solemn holiday where we keep the reality behind its existence in mind and remember the heroes we're honoring. It just didn't feel like a celebration to me this year.

All this was exacerbated by the fact that I hadn't buried Andy's ashes yet, so I had no place to visit to place flowers or a flag. I was planning that ceremony for August but wondered in that moment if I had waited too long.

A few weeks later, Father's Day was the first major holiday I "celebrated" away from Adam and Caylee in South Carolina. Here was my "Widow's Post" on that day, remembering Andy:

> Out of all the roles you had, I know being a Dad was your favorite. And you were the best I've seen. You had more natural instincts than me from the moment Adalyn was born and a child-like mind that made for the best play sessions with her. There's no denying that she is missing out on something big and amazing not having you in her life and it will never be fulfilled for her. It kills me every day that I can't change that part for her. But we promise to try. We as in our friends and family.
>
> As I sat through church outside at the park today, I felt a great deal of sadness as I witnessed myself, my sister, and my daughter all on a blanket together. Three little girls, without their Dads. But I also felt an immense gratefulness as I

looked around at the community in my corner. My friends and family. The ones who were on my porch minutes following tragic news. The ones who show up with coffee on their Father's Day to make sure I'm okay. The ones who grab my daughter and hold her when I'm having a moment. The ones whose kids give me hugs when I'm crying. The ones who have stood by my side with unwavering love and support while I have been a shell of myself. The ones who say Andy's name and tell stories. The ones that won't forget him and will make sure Adalyn knows him. The realization hit me today that these friends knew Andy longer than Adalyn did. I'm grateful for the people that will make sure Adalyn knows her Dad.

Adalyn would be unrecognizable to you now. This week at daycare, they asked for a photo of you and her for a Father's Day craft and I never found one to send because I was looking for one of you and her where she looked old enough and not like a baby anymore. And it doesn't exist.

We always had a running joke that Andy would always have one more Father's Day than I would have Mother's Day because Adalyn was born June 7. This year we tied. And I wish you were still winning.

This was also the first Father's Day both my dad and Andy were gone. Growing up, one of our greatest rituals was the convenience store 7-Eleven's annual Slurpee Day on July 11, appropriately enough. My dad would take my sister and me there, and we both got cups not just of one flavor but a whole mix of them. Blue raspberry was my favorite, and it's also Addie's. Back when I was a kid, we'd walk in, get our Slurpees mixed with every flavor and color imaginable, and leave. But these days, the crowds on Slurpee Day have gotten crazy. It's so crowded we have to battle the bodies congested before the machine to claim cups of blue raspberry for ourselves. No time anymore for the mix of rainbow colors, and the floor is so wet with spilled Slurpee concoctions that you have to pry your shoes off the linoleum to move. Despite that, it has been a nice way to remember my dad and to carry that tradition on for my daughter. The biggest difference now is she doesn't have a dad or grandpa to take her.

It wasn't long after that post, sometime between burial and 7-Eleven's annual Slurpy Day, that I had a major breakthrough I now look back on as the moment my dark winter finally came to an end. I was playing outside with Addie. I don't even remember exactly where we were, but it was a beautiful late afternoon featuring one of the most magnificent sunsets I had ever seen, the kind you can't take your eyes off.

Addie saw it too and pointed up at the sky.

"Look, Mommy, Dada made me a sunset tonight."

I was used to her running to the door every time the bell rang, saying "Dada!" But saying that made me realize she had accepted the reality that defined my dark winter. And it made me think, *Wow, if my toddler can see the light, then I can find my way out of the darkness.*

Amy and Andy's wedding on May 19, 2018.

Amy, Adalyn, and Andy in August 2023.

Andy's flag-draped coffin at his funeral.

Addie kissing "Dada's" picture.

Addie tossing dirt on Andy's grave on the day of his burial, August 2024.

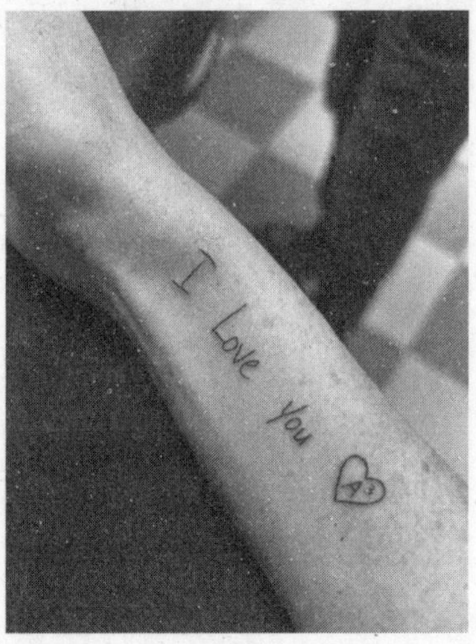

The A-cubed stands for Amy, Andy, and Addie (The "I Love You" is in Andy's handwriting).

Andy and three-month-old Adalyn on the sideline of a Central High School Falcons football game in Woodstock, Virginia in August 2022.

Amy holding Addie while holding her flag in September of 2024 on the same field as above on the night Amy presented the Colors in honor of Andy.

Addie posing in the Clarke County High School gym on Amy's (and what would have been Andy's) 10th reunion in October 2024.

A picture of freshman Andy in football regalia hanging in a Clarke County High classroom, taken during the reunion.

Halloween 2023, two days before the Humvee accident.

Halloween 2024 at Addie's daycare center.

Addie stands in front of a fence banner at the 1st Annual 5K Memorial in Andy's honor on November 2, 2024 (his first heavenly anniversary).

A finisher's medal from the Memorial 5K and Amy's bib number from the race laid atop Andy's headstone.

Addie wearing mouse ears at Disney World in January 2025.

Addie with Mickey on the same trip, standing directly in front of Tim.

CHAPTER 11

No Black

In preparing for Andy's burial on August 3, 2024, I told everyone not to wear black. Nine months had passed since his funeral, and I didn't want this to be the same kind of emotionally wrenching experience. I even told the Army's Casualty and Affairs officer, who'd be attending, not to wear his uniform. I wanted the women to come in sundresses and the men in shorts and short-sleeve shirts.

When you're young, you don't spend a lot of time talking about grave sites, so Andy and I didn't have any burial plots waiting for us. Who does in their twenties? I put so much thought into his service but none into his final resting place where Addie and I could go visit him. The only thing Andy and I settled upon was that we both wanted to be cremated. So for nine months I kept the urn with his remains unceremoniously stored in my house. And I think I was missing a big part of closure from not having buried him yet.

I found a beautiful plot in a cemetery on the grounds of the same local military academy where the Andy King Memorial 5K was set to begin and end, right off Main Street in Woodstock in the fall. It was a beautiful spot Adalyn and I could visit every weekend, perched in one of the few shady areas of the cemetery where tree branches would rustle over Andy's final resting place forever.

Looking back, I think I kept his remains for as long as I did as a way of holding on to him, not wanting to let go of this final physical piece of Andy. I don't think it's a coincidence that after we buried him, I didn't want to be in our house a minute longer and decided to rent it out right away, even though our new home in Edinburg wasn't finished yet. Not having his urn with me drove home the finality that he wasn't there anymore. I moved in with my mom a week after the burial for however long it was going to take to finish construction of my new home.

Describing the process to Adalyn was challenging. On Friday, the evening before the burial, I placed Andy's urn on a table and sat down with her on my lap so I could prepare her for what was coming.

"Your dada is in here, and we're going to bury him tomorrow," I said. "We're going to put him in the ground so we can go visit him."

Addie looked at me strangely, pointing at the urn as she said, "Dada's not in there. He's in the sky."

"You're right," I said, leaving it there because that's the way she came to accept our new life.

We wanted to leave our own marks on the urn. Addie loved my idea of putting her handprint on top of the urn, beneath which I wrote "Dada is in the sky in heaven with God," because I thought that might clarify things in her mind. Then ten minutes later, she wrapped her arms around the urn.

"My Dada's in here."

"Yes," I said, nodding, "he is."

"Let's get him out!"

It was one of those moments that made me think how everything is literal for a toddler. I had been telling Addie for months that he was in the sky and had no idea how to get across the science of cremation to her, much less the distinction between the physical and spiritual worlds. I was left speechless and, fortunately, she didn't bring it up again, but I feared how my two-year-old daughter would respond to the ceremony the next day. All I could picture was her rushing up to the grave once Andy's urn was in place, screaming, "No, no, no! Get him out!"

Pastor Nate was the only one who spoke at the burial, except for another beautifully written poem read by Andy's brother Alex. Seated on the ground, Addie rotated between eating blueberries and sucking on a lollipop as all of us approached the grave to toss dirt and white roses down atop the urn.

I couldn't help but think, *This is where we're at, this is our life. We have to have blueberries and lollipops at this funeral, because there is this toddler involved.* Addie didn't join the tradition at first. Then, at the end when Pastor Nate was wrapping up the ceremony, she walked up there by herself and started putting dirt on him, letting the soil sift through the fingers of her tiny hands.

"That's my dada," she said.

It was so wild to me that Adalyn was having her first little picnic at her dad's grave, not when she's fifty, but when she's two. It might well have been the first burial ever to feature lollipops, and that made me angry.

I'm angry at Andy too. Not because he joined the Army Reserve in the first place, not because of his death in a Humvee accident known to be among the most dangerous vehicles on the road and the least safe of any the Army uses, not because his death left me with a toddler to raise alone and a house full of broken dreams.

I'm angry because he wasn't wearing his seat belt.

In the darkest of nights, I'd toss and turn or lie in bed staring at the ceiling asking myself if things might have been different had he just done what he always did. He was seated in the back seat on the driver's side when the driver lost control of the Humvee and rolled it. The vehicle's driver's side took the major brunt of the impact.

What were you thinking, Andy? I cried out in my head more times than I could count.

I never saw him get into a vehicle without snapping his seat belt into place.

What were you thinking? You have a little girl. You have a wife.

I remember when I received the death certificate and it specified "unrestrained with ejection," meaning that Andy had been ejected from the vehicle upon impact. I didn't put the reference together at first that meant he wasn't wearing a seat belt. Later I found out that although he was ejected, his catastrophic brain injury was suffered inside the vehicle. I still don't have all the details, beyond the Virginia State Police report I was provided. The military conducts their own investigation that has taken over a year, and I still don't have their report.

Did his seat belt malfunction?

Was it broken to begin with?

I don't have all the answers or even most of them, leaving me only with questions I shouldn't have to ask.

I'm also angry at the army. As I write this at almost the two-year mark, I still have no report. No further details of that day than what is written right here. I could speculate a million things. Something doesn't feel right, that's for sure. One thing I believe is that too many of our highly skilled and trained service members with young families and their entire lives ahead of them pass away in training exercises when they shouldn't. It feels like there is so much negligence and zero accountability. Just a lot of silence.

There's nothing wrong with being angry when you've suffered the loss of a loved one. What's wrong is not having all the facts you need to fully process that loss.

Andy passed inside the vehicle from massive head trauma. As for the rest, I still have heard nothing about an inspection of the condition of his seat belt, inspection of the vehicle, qualifications of the driver, why the crash occurred, or anything else about that day.

I think back to Andy trying to get Adalyn to put that soft basketball through her kiddie hoop, how many hours he spent coaxing her into doing it and then immediately encouraging her to do it again after she finally did. I remember that and I think how he won't be around to play sports with her, to coach her soccer team and watch her score her first goal. To sit in the stands at a basketball game and watch her score her first basket outside of our living room. To work with her on her skills, kicking or tossing a ball around in the sprawling yard of the home we were building. To be the best dad he knew he could be. And the dad she needed and deserved.

I don't know if I'll ever stop being angry about that.

When Andy's phone was returned to me, I looked at his text messages. Someone had called, and he texted them back at 1:52 p.m.:

`I'm in a loud military vehicle, I'll call you in 15 minutes.`

The accident happened at 1:56. *I'll call you in 15…* Four minutes later he was dead.

I don't know if I'll ever feel at peace with putting my husband in the ground, because it feels so wrong I was put in that position in the first place. I knew I didn't want to bring Andy to the new house. I wanted his burial done before we moved. I wanted a fresh start, but that's a terrible term, because it's never really a fresh start. When Andy was alive, he was working so much he was almost never home. He spent more time in our house in Woodstock after The Call than he ever did prior to his passing. So, maybe the overwhelming desire I felt to move was him telling me it was time to get out of there.

Timmy French was at the burial. That past spring, he passed a memorial resolution through the Virginia State Senate that outlined Andy's life and how he died. That's another reason why I wanted this whole weekend to be a celebration of Andy's life.

Friday night before the burial, we all gathered at the French brothers' cabin, a place where Andy and I had shared many meals, for Timmy to present and read the memorial resolution. After a very dry summer, it rained that evening as we all gathered to remember Andy. But the following day, the day of his burial, dawned beautiful and bright. I couldn't have asked for more. I even wore those same boots I wore at our wedding and the funeral service.

I'm not sure that was a great idea, because those boots are a trigger. Just like the giant photos I'd stored in our shed after the funeral back in November that I pulled all out again, along with Andy's memorabilia and awards. The experience took me back nine months in time and left me feeling exactly as I did the day of the funeral.

Even with that familiar flood of feelings surging back, the burial was exactly how I pictured it. I posted this on Facebook about the whole experience:

> As I reflect back on this past weekend, all I can think about is how lucky we are that Andy made it so easy to remember him. Nostalgia overcame me this weekend as we pulled out photos, flags, Helena swag, and even Andy's truck making an appearance.
>
> On Friday, we had a celebration of life where over one hundred family and friends from multiple states showed up, as Timmy French read and presented the memorial resolution passed through the Senate of Virginia in Andy's honor. The whole night it felt like Andy was just around the corner, especially as the much-needed rain poured.
>
> On Saturday morning, we had a beautiful burial service where Adalyn laid dirt on her dada and said goodbye to the last physical piece of him. She understood better than all of us when she reminded me that it wasn't him, and that he was in the sky with heaven and God. The little person that loses the most from this is the one who somehow accepts it the most.
>
> I am eternally grateful for the friends and family who continually show up for Addie and I. Everyone had a good laugh at me saying it would

> be a small event over the last few months as I was planning it. There is no such thing as small in Andy's world.
>
> We laughed through tears and enjoyed many Andy stories throughout the weekend. It was a piece of closure many of us needed.
>
> Grief is the price we pay for love.

I felt so great over the weekend but sank really low when everyone went back home on Sunday, leaving me surrounded by cards and flowers once again. I should have gone back to South Carolina with Adam and Caylee instead of returning home. Lesson learned.

Speaking of triggers, on the Friday before the burial, I went to a local florist to get Adalyn a little bouquet to carry to the burial and a small display to place behind the headstone. I hadn't been to a flower shop since before Andy died, and it smelled like the funeral home. I remember approaching the door the night of the service, and I could smell the flowers even before I went inside.

I walked in and there were so many flowers on display. I asked someone, "Are there a bunch of services going on?"

"No," the person told me, "these are all Andy's."

I hate the smell of flowers now. I never want to smell flowers again.

In the wake of the burial, I began having these strange thoughts—call them fantasies, or an alternate reality—in which Andy survived the crash but was badly injured. I imagined him beating the odds to make a full recovery, with Addie and me by his side the whole time.

Because he's Andy King.

But my new extended family would have still rallied to our side, his brothers and their wives, and our relationship would be forged in the same stone it is today thanks to a near-death experience instead of a death experience. If only that scenario had played out....

Soon after the burial, one of Andy's friends and suppliers from work, Daniel, invited Addie and me out to his farm to see his cows and have lunch with his wife and kids. We drove over a few weeks later and were buzzing around on an ATV taking in the scenery, Addie smiling up a storm the whole way, especially when we drew up close to the cows.

"Do you think Adalyn would like to sit on my lap and work the steering wheel?" he asked me.

Lots of thoughts went through my mind in that moment, but only a single word emerged.

"Sure!" I said. "You want to drive the ATV, Addie?"

She started bouncing in my lap. We stopped and Daniel took her in his lap, and moments later, her little hands were squeezing the wheel. I don't think I've ever seen a bigger smile on my daughter's face, and all I could think of was how Andy would have loved this, only with Adalyn in his lap instead, driving for the first time.

Since that was no longer possible, this was the next best thing.

CHAPTER 12

Colors

Adalyn's first football game was a Central Falcons home game on September 2, 2022, when she was just three months old. Andy was so pumped that she was out there on the field with him on one of the nights he was running the chains, it was probably one of the only times he actually said, "Take my picture!"

He is beaming in that photo. This little memory that seemed so insignificant at the time now forms a great bookend to a beautiful Friday night on September 6, 2024, when the school's athletic director and former head football coach asked me to present the colors in a pregame ceremony prior to the playing of our national anthem.

It was a surreal experience to say the least, with Addie attending her second football game, this time to honor her dada while wearing a Falcons jersey.

How cool is that, right?

Adalyn not only came to the game, she participated in the ceremony itself, along with her two uncles, Andy's brothers Adam and Alex.

Friday night football is a time-honored tradition in the little town of Woodstock. The temperature was in the seventies at kickoff with minimal humidity, perfect weather to enjoy an evening outdoors. The sun popped out of the clouds as it was setting over the field, with the Blue Ridge Mountains rising in the background. Many in my position might look at that as a metaphor for my own life since The Call, but for me the whole night was anything but that.

Standing at the fifty-yard line, I was facing the jam-packed stands set back a bit from the field atop a hill. Lawn chairs dotted the grass between the fence line and those stands, people enjoying a beautiful evening under the lights that began with Addie's Uncle Alex holding her while I held a large American flag. Of course, for Addie it's "Dada's flag," and she clung to hers all night, except for the times she let her cousins and a couple of the classmates from preschool who came to take a turn waving it. Watching her share the flag that way brought a lump to my throat, because I realized she was sharing Andy, letting the other kids hold the little piece of him that was hers. And she told them all that: "It's my Dada's flag."

"Andy King and his wife Amy moved to Woodstock, Virginia, in November of 2020," the public address announcer began. "They enjoyed the community and decided Woodstock would be their home. Andy enjoyed farming and worked as an agricultural salesman for Helena. Andy eventually became an avid supporter of Central Football and joined our chain crew for Friday night football games. Andy loved his country and served as a captain in the Army Reserve. While serving in the Reserve, Andy passed away tragically in an army training accident on November 2, 2023. Andy King was twenty-seven years old. Tonight, presenting our nation's colors in remembrance of Captain Andy King, are his wife Amy, their beautiful daughter Adalyn, as well as his two brothers Alex and Adam King. Ladies and gentlemen, can we get a big round of applause for Captain Andy King and the entire King family…."

The crowd erupted in applause and cheers.

"At this time, would everyone please rise and remove your hats and honor America with the playing of our national anthem."

Most of the crowd rose to give Andy one last cheer. I don't think many of them actually knew Andy or even knew who he was, beyond the guy who worked the first-down chain crew with him. Tonight, that chore fell on a couple of students, and it was strange to look down on the field to see someone else doing it.

It was an emotional experience, as was the whole weekend. Adam and Caylee came up with the twins, joined by Alex and Lauren, who had relocated to Alex's new navy posting in Washington, DC, which made it an easy trip for them too. The last few times we had all been together here had been for Andy's funeral and, more recently, his burial. So it felt so nice to get together for a normal weekend, something positive. It still fostered a lot of emotions, though, thanks to this being the first visit where Charlie and Henry joined their parents. Andy's two brothers presenting the colors with me was not only appropriate, it provided the excuse we needed to gather as a family. I had shirts made for Charlie and Henry too, so they'd feel a part of things, and I wouldn't have traded the sight of all three kids wearing their football jerseys for anything.

Coincidentally, there was a beautiful old farmhouse on four acres of land in Edinburg directly across the street from where

I was building the house Addie and I were planning to call our new home. The owners were away for an extended period, so they turned the place into an Airbnb. My sister-in-law Caylee had arranged to stay there over that weekend in large part because they figured I'd be into my new house by then, only the road separating us, but construction delays waylaid that.

"It's a perfect location for us," she told one of the owners, after explaining the purpose of their visit, "right across the street from where my sister-in-law is building her house."

"What's her name?" the woman asked.

"Amy King."

"Oh," the woman responded, "I've heard about her. Please give her my phone number. My husband and I would love to welcome her to the neighborhood."

It turned out that woman was a therapist, just like Caylee, and had a six-month-old baby. Both she and her husband serve in the military and were currently stationed in Hawaii, explaining why their house was available. I continue to be amazed by the overlapping, random things that keep popping up in my life and was struck by how much our family had in common with these total strangers Caylee was renting a house from.

Since my house wasn't ready yet, Addie and I actually ended up staying at the Airbnb as well, and I could tell she was as excited as I was. While she was on the porch swing the next morning I asked her who was coming over later. Normally she'd say "grammy" or "auntie," but instead she said, "My dada!"

She's never said that before, not even once. "No," I told her gently, "he's not coming here. Where is he?"

"Oh yeah," she answered in toddler talk. "He's in the sky."

We left it there, but I couldn't get Addie saying that out of my head. It was definitely strange and it made me wonder, given that we were celebrating Andy together as a family in a way that never would have happened if it hadn't been for the accident. For those who don't believe in coincidence, it certainly makes you wonder...and smile. There's a quote attributed to the French philosopher Pierre Teilhard de Chardin that goes, "We are not physical beings having a spiritual experience; we are spiritual beings having a physical experience." The more I think about it, the more that makes perfect sense.

Andy's brothers and their families were so grateful to be included in the colors ceremony, as well as the weekend as a whole. They feared that, like so many widows on Facebook, there would no longer be any connection between them and Adalyn and me. We were all that was keeping Andy alive for them, in memory and spirit, and they didn't want to lose that any more than I wanted to lose their love and friendship. I also didn't want my family to stop growing bigger. Nothing would bring Andy back, but having his brothers and their families in my life was as close to that as I could come. Family shouldn't mean less after suffering a loss, it should mean more.

"I feel I don't deserve you guys," I said to Caylee at one point, "because of how our relationship was before."

"Are you kidding me?" she asked me, wide-eyed. "We're the ones who are clinging to you."

We were bonded by the strongest force imaginable: Andy. And maybe "clinging" is as good a way to describe it as any. When I was on that football field for the colors, and when I'm with Andy's friends or his coworkers from Helena, I cling to that because it's when I feel him the strongest. My heart breaks for the people who don't have something like that.

Our weekend at the farmhouse was joyous and fun, so different from what we shared at Andy's funeral and burial service. My brother and sister came too, making it truly a family affair that was made even more special by the fact that they had never met Charlie and Henry before. We were truly filling up each other's lives, opening new doors instead of closing them.

We grilled fillet mignon for dinner Saturday night, just like Andy would have done. Of course, who was going to cook them, since he wasn't here? I asked my brother Vincent if he would stand in, and he did a great job that Andy would have been proud of. We had a campfire at night, ate s'mores, and walked across the street to my not-quite-finished new house, where we had coffee on the deck the next morning. The view of the mist-shrouded Blue Ridge Mountains in the distance looked lifted off a postcard, almost as if they were welcoming me to the neighborhood with a sample of how all my days would soon start. My yard consists of five completely fenced-in acres, so the twins and Addie were having a ball running along the fence line with the tireless energy of toddlers.

One of the first things Andy fell in love with about this property was that view. From the deck where we shared coffee and stories, it seemed like the world stretched beyond the mountains, never ending, which was the way we felt about our lives together.

Being at midfield for the ceremony and then in the stands for the rest of the time we were there stoked memories of high school, when Andy and I started dating. How many games had I watched him play for the Clarke County Eagles? I remember being there on Friday nights, giddy over watching my boyfriend suiting up at linebacker while already looking forward to seeing him after the game. I don't think I've ever been more in the moment than back then, because in high school, all of those moments seem crucial. You don't appreciate at the time how incredible it is not to worry about anything beyond your next game, test, or kiss. Watching the Woodstock Central Falcons play made me realize how much I missed such simpler times that vanish in the complications of college, career, marriage, parenting, grief. When opportunity allowed, my gaze would stray to the high school students gathered with their friends in and out of the stands, enjoying those times as much as I had. And I thought more than once how any of the girls could have been me, and any of the boys could have been Andy. I watched Addie having a blast just running around, not thinking beyond eating some more of her ice cream and showing off her dada's flag. That's the ultimate example of living in the moment, not thinking about what happened before or what's coming next.

I think what I found most gratifying about the evening was the repeated mention of the Andy King Memorial 5K over the PA system. I found that to be a great gesture and, even more, a bridge between the Andy who would have been working the chain crew at this game and where he is now. That meant the game wasn't just about celebrating Andy's memory but also supporting that memory going forward. He may be physically gone, but that doesn't mean a lot of good can't be accomplished in his name.

That evening left me pondering not just the high school experience we shared but also the college one. We actually didn't start at Virginia Tech together. I attended the University of Florida my freshman year before leaving after one semester. I came home because it just wasn't for me and took classes at a local community college that spring and summer. I worked my butt off and saved a whole bunch of money while figuring out next steps. Andy told me to check out the agribusiness field that he was studying at Tech, and I ended up meeting with the woman whose family owned the farm Andy had worked on through college, Frenda, who quickly became a close friend to me. Speaking with her stimulated my interest in agribusiness, and I formally transferred to join Andy at Virginia Tech to pursue a degree on that career track as well.

Tech hadn't really been Andy's first choice either. His prowess on the football field earned him interest from at least one Division II school where he could have continued his football career. But the school wasn't offering a full scholarship, and his parents weren't of a mind to help out at all. That's why he signed up for ROTC and enrolled at Virginia Tech. It meant being part of the Tech's Corps of Cadets, a pretty rigid program much more rigorous than ROTC programs at other schools. He had to wear his uniform all the time through the entirety of freshman year. He couldn't go out on weekends without permission, which he also needed to seek for any number of otherwise normal college activities.

On the one hand, I hold great resentment toward Andy's parents for not supporting him at the end of his senior year. That's why he ended up joining the army, and if he hadn't joined the army, The Call never would have come. On the other hand, I don't think Andy ever would have grown into the man he became without the Corps of Cadets at Virginia Tech. That experience changed him at his core. It tested him to the breaking point and came to define the essence of the man I would later marry.

During that magical Friday evening of football, I couldn't help but reflect on the fact that my tenth high school reunion, and Andy's too, was coming the following month on October 27. I hadn't seen any of my friends and classmates from Clarke County since the funeral, and prior to that, it had been ten years. I was the first in my class to get married, have a child, and now, become a widow, the only one in attendance who checked those three boxes for sure. A few months ago, I never would have been ready for that, but it's one of those things I know Andy would have done, and that made attending our tenth reunion another way of honoring him.

Even if it was hard, the experience would be worth it, and I knew just what I was going to show my classmates so it felt like he was with me.

PART THREE

THE TREES

Four stems climbed upwards toward the sun
Independent they rose, though from one they begun
Every so often, the shoots merged and twisted
But remained their own tree-lings, convergence resisted
A loose wicker framework built up over time
Loose but supportive, through the rain and the shine
Each tree rose up, leaves stretched to the sun
Different colors and shapes, yet still part of the one.

These trees grew taller, became part of the forest
Though each limb often felt that connection was porous
One limb spread itself outward, stretching towards others
Interacting with neighbors as if they were brothers
The limb used its strength to make known its presence
It did not smother its neighbors, but instead shared its essence
Twisting, entwining and joining the forest
This tree lent its voice to the rest of the chorus.

By force and by virtue, this tree made itself known
By building up others, it built its own throne
These green things it touched became greener in turn
Other green things leaned closer, for its influence they yearned
One stray shot of lightning on a cloudless blue day
And this great knotted tree was taken away
The forest will mourn for the tree it had known
While no longer here, it will always be home.

Alex King
(reprinted with permission)

CHAPTER 13

High School Sweethearts

Believe it or not, my getting involved in my ten-year high school reunion began at Andy's funeral. My friend and our class president, Jasmine, came, along with a number of my classmates, and most of them also attended the visitation the night before. That truly warmed my heart, stoking the best memories from my four years at Clarke County High. I suddenly felt nostalgic.

"I think we need to do a ten-year reunion," I said to Jasmine, when I was finally able to talk with her after the funeral.

"Great idea!" she said.

"Then let's plan it. Will you help me?"

Technically, as class president, that was her job. But I was school president at the same time back then, so there was a lot of overlap in our duties, which meant we were used to working together. That might seem like a strange cause to take up barely a week after The Call. I knew, though, that two more of our classmates had passed away before Andy. And my primary reason for involving myself in the reunion was to make sure we paid proper respect to all three now and honor their memories.

We started a Facebook page for the Clarke County High School Class of 2014. We were part of a class numbering about 150 and had no idea what to expect from a turnout standpoint, but we decided to keep it simple to attract the most people possible. I had no idea when we selected Sunday, October 27, as the date, how much more I'd have going on that week. That I'd be moving into my new house two days later on October 29 or running the Andy King Memorial 5K on November 2, with Halloween, the last night I ever spent with Andy, sandwiched in the middle.

Keeping things simple meant starting the day at one o'clock with a tour of the new high school we'd moved into after our sophomore year to see all the improvements and walk those halls again. Then, the plan was to gather at a new brewery a few miles away. It was owned by parents of a few of our classmates, which made it perfect, except for one small thing:

It wasn't open yet.

Luckily, though, the owners loved the idea of doing a soft opening with us.

We ended up with fifty people registered, including spouses and kids, and I have to tell you, spending an hour back inside Clarke County High School was really something. Nothing from the shine of the linoleum floors to the smell that hangs in the hallways had changed. I think I remembered my locker number, but not the combination. At one point, we stopped in the classroom where Andy and I had taken business classes together for years with Ms. Elson, who still teaches there. Those were probably the classes we gained the most from, because they helped get us to where we were in our careers. We sat next to each other in this very classroom, which felt surreal, since it looked exactly the same. I'd give Andy a hug or kiss before class, and Ms. Elson would be standing there, smiling…before telling us to move along.

Ms. Astin was the teacher leading the school tour. Andy and I knew her well also. Adalyn took time out from running down the halls to claim a desk for herself when we got to her classroom. Ms. Astin was the perfect choice to lead the tour because she had dedicated a wall of her long-time classroom to what she calls her Hall of Fame, consisting of wallet-size photos of students she'd taught over the years—mostly athletes, because Ms. Astin remains Clarke County High's cheerleading coach to this day. She pulled me to the wall and showed me Andy's picture proudly displayed there, posed in full football regalia. I brought Addie over and showed it to her.

"That's your dada!" I announced.

I'm not sure it registered, since she was a bit overstimulated by all the people around her and being in an unfamiliar place. I was so glad I'd brought her, because there weren't a lot of high school sweethearts in our class, so Addie is definitely a Class of 2014 baby and much deserving of a seat at the table—or, in this case, at one of the big kids' desks. She was fascinated by all the lockers, one of which I stuffed her into to play peekaboo. It was weird to see her on the premises of a place where Andy and I had shared so many memories. Every time I looked at her standing in this place or that, I pictured Andy standing there as he no doubt had ten years before. Jasmine has a little girl about the same age, so she and Addie ended up traipsing around together. Which left me reflecting on the fact that in a dozen years or so, Addie would be doing that in her own high school. Only she'd be able to read the time on the wall clocks and numbers on her locker.

Ms. Elson is one of two teachers, the other being Ms. Campbell, I've seen twice since graduating: once at my dad's funeral and then again at Andy's. Ms. Campbell retired, so her classroom is no longer the same, but I still expected to see her around the next corner.

In preparation for this day, I reached out to the families of those other two members of the Class of 2014 who passed, which allowed me to reconnect with my dear friend Sam's mother. I so admired her because she never shied away from the fact that Sam died from his addiction. Here's the opening line from his obituary:

> [He] passed away unexpectedly…after a brave and hard fought battle with addiction.

Like me, Sam's mom Kathy isn't afraid to say things out loud, and I love her for that. She really wanted people to understand that he had a disease he fought every day of his life. I had a really long visit with Sam's mom and dad in their home a few weeks before the reunion. At one point, I was sitting on the front porch with her as we reminisced and talked about Sam and Andy. It's crazy how grief will connect you to people you never thought you would cross paths with again. She had a hard time when I asked for photos of Sam for the memorial display at our ten-year reunion, because there weren't many pictures of him from those last years of his life. The majority of the photos, the ones we ended up displaying, were of him as a younger child, in stark contrast to Andy, who really struggled as a child, explaining why all the best photos of him were the most recent, the ones taken closest to The Call. In fact, I remember as we were gathering photos for Andy's memorial slideshow at the funeral, I was so sad seeing photos of him as a kid, knowing how much he had to overcome when he was younger. Not only was Sam's mother not able to plan a proper funeral because of COVID, she never got to see her son realize his full potential, and that made me sad.

Kathy and I actually had more in common when it came to my dad's death, not Andy's. When I spoke to Kathy, she told me that she felt Sam was too sensitive and good for this Earth. I related to that immediately because I felt the same way about my dad. That connected us on an even deeper level, and I was struck by her courage in speaking the unvarnished truth in the hope it would help others. When my dad died by suicide, we never publicly revealed it, but if we had to do things all over again, I like to think we would follow the example set by Kathy and showcase his bravery in fighting a sickness that ultimately claimed his life.

The reunion was a big test for me. I'd spent the past year making sure I was not shying away from grief. I could have avoided the weddings I attended and this reunion too, because I didn't want to bear the burden of being the eight-hundred-pound gorilla in the room that everyone was whispering about when they thought I wasn't watching. Doing the opposite of that, staying in the moment, was a vital ingredient of my healing process, and it helped me accept the new reality I was facing instead of clinging to a life that was gone.

It also helped that a lot of the people who attended the reunion were at Andy's visitation, as well as his funeral. Interestingly enough, I didn't wear my wedding ring, and the fact is I stopped wearing it not long after Andy's funeral. Taking it off further helped me solidify the reality of my situation. Everyone was immensely supportive, and there was a good mix of remembering Andy from the past but also talking about the present and future.

Seeing my high school classmates inevitably led to comparisons. There were no other widows present, some people had two or three kids by now, and some were just beginning new and exciting marriages. It made me think of my situation and how much I craved a full family unit again, one where Adalyn would get siblings. The man who gives us that will have to realize he's not a stepdad sharing Adalyn with her real father on weekends and holidays. It won't be a part-time job. That man will need to be a full-time father for someone else's child, which is a high bar.

I have so much more confidence in myself than I did a year ago. I know who I am more than I ever have, as well as having come to grips with who I was at the time of The Call. Being forced to be a single full-time mom allows for a lot of reflection. And losing your husband at twenty-seven forces you to reidentify yourself. The fact remains Andy and I were in the midst of a very difficult time that most young couples with newborns or toddlers face. Change is evitable, and the marriages that last normally cast the man and woman as willing partners in accepting the fact that they're not happy-go-lucky high school or college sweethearts or newlyweds anymore. The truth is, while I miss my husband a lot, sometimes I miss my best friend and father of my child more. There was so much left behind in terms of our marriage that I had to reconcile alone.

As I said, I follow a lot of widows' Facebook group pages. Their rawest posts focus on the fact that death, especially a tragic and sudden one, leaves other mourners to place victims like Andy on a pedestal. I remember once hearing that it was important to love someone, warts and all. Well, mourners never consider the warts-and-all of a relationship. There's only sunshine in their view, no clouds. They don't know about the fights Andy and I had over this or that, or the struggles we endured. Even after a year, Andy remained on a pedestal, and I'm not saying he didn't earn it, but it made it very difficult for them to accept or understand any kind of complex feelings I was having. It is such a complicated grief. I not only have to process his death, I have to process an entire marriage that had damaging parts for both of us on my own. Obviously I didn't want him gone, but his absence made me have to confront hard parts of our marriage that we never did, and reflect on how both of us could have done better. Being forced to stand on my own two feet has made me process the portions of our marriage which took a toll on both of us that I needed to heal from as well.

After the tour of the school, we all convened at the brewery. The setting couldn't have been more perfect. Imagine an establishment built in the middle of a rolling meadow with cows grazing in the postcard-perfect scene beyond, surrounded by mountain views on all sides. The owners built it on the land of their cattle farm.

From the outside, the brewery evokes visions of an old-school Southern roadhouse, with a peaked roof and a covered porch that stretches the entire length of the building. It's a lot bigger on the inside than it looks from the outside.

It was the ideal spot to share stories and catch up on where everyone was in life. The gathering wasn't fancy or elaborate. Everybody just ordered and paid for themselves. We had a cake, and Jasmine said a few words welcoming everyone and acknowledging the three classmates we were missing. It was just nice to be in the company of so many people who'd been part of my life, as well as my life with Andy.

My final takeaway was watching Addie interact with all the adults showering her with attention. Normally she's pretty shy, but on this day she really opened up, the life of the party. I swear, it was almost like she was channeling Andy and, incredibly, she seemed to get along best with our classmates who had been closest to him. She wanted them to play with the toys I had brought along for her, and she kept gobbling down cupcakes. It took whole napkins to wipe the frosting off her mouth and cheeks. I remember thinking wouldn't it be nice if life's messes were as easy to clean up.

CHAPTER 14

The Good Dinosaur

Today is the final goodbye of our home. Tomorrow, a new family will move in and fill this place with new memories. I wish I was leaving here as a family of 3. We bought this home in 2020. This home was the gateway to finding our church, meeting our best friends, and starting our family. This porch used to be the backdrop for photos of a family of 3 over the last nine months, it became a place that I sat and grieved. As my friends came up my driveway one by one yesterday to wish this house farewell, it was reminiscent of when I saw them walk up one by one to hold me on this porch on the worst day of my life. We've celebrated here and grieved here. This is the last place I saw Andy. Adalyn and I hugged him and waved goodbye at this front door as we watched him pull out of the driveway for the last time as we said, "See ya Sunday." This house has been so heavy the last 9 months. Although I am more than ready to leave it behind, I wish I was leaving it in the same glory as we started. Not much good happened here over the last 9 months, but I will always hold this home close to my heart. I started my family here, and I said goodbye to my husband here.

Proverbs 3:5-6 (NIV)
"Trust in the Lord with all your heart and lean not on your own understanding; in all your ways submit to him, and he will make your paths straight."

I made that Facebook post the morning of our move to my mother's in Winchester in September of 2024, a temporary stopover until the house I was building in Edinburg was ready. I had no choice other than to leave, because I'd already rented out the house in Woodstock on the expectation my new one would be finished. I couldn't have felt better about moving, because the heaviness that settled into the home from the moment of The Call never dissipated and became an anchor for my emotions, keeping me from moving forward.

The front lawn was the worst reminder of all. Andy was really good at landscaping, so he kept up the grass and flower beds meticulously. Always fertilized and mulched. The first thing he would do at every house we lived was create mulch beds and plant a red maple tree. That was his thing, not mine, and besides visits from a local landscaper to mow it, the yard hadn't been touched much in the ten months since Andy's death. So, the day we moved it was the worst it ever looked, overgrown with lavender climbing over the mailbox. I remember crying when I saw a dandelion show up amid the grass, because I had never seen a single one sprout on Andy's vigilant watch.

That final moment was tough on Addie, because she didn't understand why the moving men were removing our furniture.

"That's my chair," she said. "That's my couch."

Good thing she was excited about us staying with my mom. She must have seen that as a kind of great adventure, and I'm convinced she fully grasped the notion that we weren't coming back. She adjusted quickly to the point that when I picked her up at school, she didn't ask about the house or "going home" at all. She had other priorities now.

"Let's go see Grammy!"

She said that virtually every day, and that's what we did for nearly two months, until it was time to move into our new home on October 29, once it was finally finished.

Our new home in Edinburg, ten miles from Woodstock on the west side of Route 81, might have originally started out as a garage, but it evolved into a comfortable space that exceeded my expectations, at least initially. I didn't feel weird about being here without Andy, and I didn't miss the house we shared for our final three years together. I wasn't sad about being in this new place, which represented the first major thing I had done that Andy wasn't an indelible part of. Sure, we picked out the land and planned everything together. Then those plans changed. Instead of the big house we intended to build, I downsized to this smaller space that I felt content with at the time.

The sun rises over the Blue Ridge and sets over the Allegheny Mountains. The whole house had 360-degree views of the mountains. It was beautiful and peaceful. There were even six horses from a neighboring farm that came up to our fence every morning, and I could see them outside the window in the kitchen section of the ground floor.

"Where's the horses, Mommy?" Addie always asked me.

She loved them, and the feeling must have been mutual because they always approached when she ran ahead of me across a part of our five acres to make her daily greeting. One morning it was so cold, the horses had blankets draped over their backs.

"Look, Mommy," Addie said, pointing, "they have their coats on."

The house featured an open floor plan. The living room and dining area were larger than I had envisioned, enough so that there was plenty of room for the Murphy bed that rests inside a tailored cut-out in the wall, until I eased it down every night to sleep. A staircase led to an upstairs loft where Addie has staked out her own space. Coming from a ranch house, the staircase leading up to it fascinated her, and there was no shortage of drama when she climbed or descended them. The first few days she kept telling me she wanted to go back to "Grammy's house." But within a week or so, when I picked her up at school, Addie said she wanted to go to "Mommy's house."

And she continued to talk about Andy a lot. She loved looking at the moon and talking about that too. So, it was no longer just "Dada's in the sky" anymore. It was "Dada's in the moon and Heaven is in the moon."

It's funny, but we never took time to look at the moon or the night sky in Woodstock. It was so crystal clear at our new house, and the stars looked close enough to reach up and touch.

Not all that long before, I struggled through the whirlwind of decisions confronting me about the next stage of my life. Should I stop building the house? Should I move back to Winchester where my family lives? Should I move to South Carolina where

Adam and Caylee live? I didn't know what to do. Maybe that indecision was a good thing, because it kept me from rushing into anything. I took my time, kept building the house, and as the weeks and months passed, things grew clearer as the fog of grief started to abate. This house, at least the property on which it rests, was the last thing Andy was directly involved in with me. Everything else in my life, from this point on, would be new.

And yet, things that remind me of Andy were everywhere. Just a mile down the road at the end of my driveway was one of his biggest customers, and he serviced just about all the other farms I passed no matter which way I went. That included some on the way to drop Adalyn off at school. Despite the move, that left me in a bit of a funk because I didn't have to pass anything familiar when I was living with my mom in Winchester, and it was starting to feel impossible to move forward so long as I stayed in the area.

The town of Woodstock was exactly what I needed at the time of my life when Andy and I happened upon it. The people, the church, the friends—everything. It was the perfect place to start and raise a family. Now, Woodstock seemed part and parcel of the heaviness I tried to escape when I moved out of the home Andy and I bought together. Moving into the new space so close to Woodstock made me realize that it wasn't just the house that was weighing me down, it was also the town itself. It felt like I was constantly passing through hard memories everywhere I went. Our spot at the café, shopping in the only grocery store there, passing by places he used to work, dropping Adalyn off at the day care. It is the most bizarre feeling to suddenly not recognize or identify with your entire life and routine. This life I was living wasn't for me without Andy in it. A small town can be both a blessing and a curse, and Woodstock had been so much the former to me before it evolved into the latter.

I felt like an entirely different person than I did at this time last year. Sometimes, I found myself valuing peace over companionship and just wanted to be around *me.* I had grown and evolved since The Call in my own way. It was a huge milestone for me to *want* to be alone. To want my space and privacy. To be able to sit in my grief sometimes and not feel like I needed to go out and distract myself from it. I wanted to prioritize quality time with my daughter and my family. I wanted to laugh and have fun again and not be weighed down by all the subconscious memories that came as I passed by all the familiar places we used to frequent.

At least with the move out to Edinburg, I took an entirely different route when I drove Addie to school, and the part I loved the most was when I picked her up in the evenings. It used to be so depressing to make that drive to our old home. We'd pass the park where we used to go, the fairgrounds where she'd spun around on her first amusement park ride and where Andy's funeral was held, and so many places where Andy and I would stop in regularly. We even passed the route where we went trick-or-treating his last Halloween. Now, the ride home was absolutely peaceful and beautiful. This time of year, I watched the sun setting and I didn't pass a single landmark like that on the way.

That new route became symbolic of my new identity. It took me a whole year to find myself, figure out who I really was. And sometimes that can take longer or shorter for people, and all of it is okay. I don't think you can ever be prepared for something like this, but I do think losing my dad so traumatically and suddenly gave me a perspective that helped me. I knew life could change on a dime, and now I knew it could happen twice. And I knew it could do it again, so I had to make the most out of the time I had there. For Andy. For my dad. For Addie.

As I was building my house, you might say, I was also rebuilding myself, which is why I was excited to get out there. We kind of grew up together. When I was living in my old house, I dreaded getting up in the morning. Everything felt so heavy. Since moving in to the new house, I became more excited to get up and start my day. Instead of waiting for Adalyn to wake up, I got up before her. Some mornings, the sun streaming through the windows woke me at the crack of dawn, so I took the dogs out and walked the property while the sun rose. I never realized how different a physical space could make you feel.

One thing that didn't change in the new house was Addie watching her Disney movies. Lately, her favorite had become *The Good Dinosaur*. It was one of the most depressing films of all time, because the dad dies in front of the kid dinosaur in the beginning and then his mom dies at the end. Addie watched it, literally, every day. I sometimes wondered if it was what grief processing looked like for a two-year-old.

"Oh, he lost his daddy, he lost his mommy," she said every time she watched the movie.

"But is he okay?" I managed to ask her.

"Yeah, he's okay," she told me.

I finally realized that was my way of asking Addie if she was okay, and her way of telling me that she was.

CHAPTER 15

Pumpkins on the Porch

One of the clearest lasting memories I have of those emotionally devastating moments I had immediately after receiving The Call was sitting on my porch, head in my hands between my knees, trying to make sense of the reality that was just beginning to sink in. I'd turn an empty gaze occasionally to the left or the right of me and see the fall pumpkins scattered on my porch.

Since November 2, 2023, I've dealt with a few triggers that bring the worst moments of that experience back to me. Onrushing ambulances with sirens screaming for one, car crashes in general for another, to the point where I can feel my insides seize up whenever I see approaching flashing lights on a highway with traffic slowed or stalled by a car accident. Other triggers include the cool, crisp air of fall or the sight of fallen leaves...

And pumpkins.

Last fall, I never actually took my own displayed pumpkins in. The volunteers from Woodstock's auxiliary fire department and friends did that months later at the same time they wondrously decorated my house for Christmas. It was almost as if I didn't want to touch them.

Halloween was such a special occasion for Andy that the first one without him came with its own set of challenges, not the least of which was the endless line of pumpkins sitting atop every single porch I walked by, drove past, or viewed from afar. The last thing I wanted to do was celebrate Halloween in 2024 as we had in 2023 just days before the accident. I didn't want to take part in the long lines of trick-or-treaters assembled along the streets of Woodstock, dressed in every conceivable costume, being shepherded from house to house by an army of flash-light-wielding parents.

This was especially important for the state of my psyche and spirit. I had recently come across some photos taken during that trip to the Bahamas. Although I was smiling, you could see the sadness in my eyes. I compared those to some pictures on my phone from nine months later, around the time of that high school football game where I presented the colors, and couldn't help but notice the difference. I was smiling in these shots too, only this time the sadness was gone. I found the transformation striking, and the last thing I wanted to do was let any old triggers, like an endless sea of pumpkins on porches and trick-or-treating in Woodstock, set me back.

I skipped a lot of main Halloween events a year after The Call. The town held something called Trick-or-Treating on Main Street on the Saturday prior, where all the business along Woodstock's main drag give out candy to the parade of kids who went door-to-door. Different businesses offered special features like a magician or face-painting, and even the fire department got into the act with all kinds of games within view of a big fire engine. Andy and I took Addie to that her first two Halloweens, starting when she was just four months old. While there were plenty of traditions I planned to keep up, this wasn't going to be one of them.

In the past, Halloween for me had been a whole-month affair. This year, though, I wanted it to just be one day. Addie was Minnie Mouse in 2024, continuing our Disney theme from the prior year, and I didn't even find her costume until the night before. And it was a dress-up outfit my sister had bought her months earlier. I did the absolute bare minimum, and that was okay.

The day itself started with Addie's day care center hosting a great event called Trunk-or-Treat. A circular drive enclosed the building on which staff, parents, and visitors parked, but that morning, a collection of cars was tightly packed in a semicircle, some of them decorated and all with their trunks raised to reveal more decorations and candy. Starting with the youngest, the kids filed out the back door one class at a time to walk along the half circle with festive candy bags in hand. I don't think the youngest had much of an idea what was going on, no more than Addie did last year. This year, when it came to her class's turn, she walked right up to the first car.

"Trick or treat!" she said, the first time she'd ever said that, and I tried not to think about the fact that she had no memory of going out trick-or-treating with her father last year or that this was yet another milestone he'd missed and would have especially loved.

So, it was kind of like she was experiencing the whole thing in her Minnie Mouse costume for the first time. I was amazed at how big she had gotten, after being Cinderella the year before. A great way to start the day, but I had no desire to end it as we had last year, with Addie joining a million other kids holding those glow sticks that lit the night for as far as the eye could see.

Instead, I got together with the Six Friends and planned something entirely unique. Josh and Amanda had recently moved to an older, hilly neighborhood lined with stately Victorian and colonial homes that normally kept their lights off and didn't give out any Halloween candy.

This year, though, Josh and Amanda called a bunch of their neighbors to ask if they'd make an exception for a dozen or so kids, and ten said they'd be more than happy to oblige. So we formed our own tiny kid convoy, led by Josh on his bike pulling a covered dolly with his kids inside. I was pushing Addie in her stroller, and a couple of the other parents had strollers as well. The older kids, seven or eight years old, who came along for the ride were probably a little disappointed they weren't with the rest of the town's kids cluttering the sidewalks and streets as we had last year. The houses all had big manicured yards, which meant they were spaced farther apart, appearing even more distant from each other because the neighborhood's hilly streets were lined with dips and rises that kind of symbolized the past year in my life.

Our little group even had glow sticks, just like last year. They just didn't glow as bright or as far, but from up close the picture was exactly the same. I didn't think at the time how this was such an appropriate scene, given how my world had shrunk in the aftermath of Halloween last year. The night last year had been cold and windy, in stark contrast to this, where the temperature touched eighty during the day and clung to the seventies after the sun set.

Addie was still too young to eat most of the candy she collected at the front doors of all ten houses. Even last year, Andy and I threw away just about all the contents of her plastic pumpkin except for a single Reese's Peanut Butter Cup he and her shared. I continued that tradition with Addie this year, splitting one with her, which was nice and soft, easy for her to eat.

She walked up to the front doors of every single house with me, something she had done a bit last year too because Andy had been adamant about giving her the "full experience." Even though she had no memory of that evening, she looked like a veteran clutching the handle of her little pumpkin candy holder like she was never going to let go.

"Trick or treat!" she'd say, gaining confidence with each ring of the doorbell.

Watching Addie, I realized this night wasn't really about the candy since she couldn't eat most of it yet anyway. And I also realized the limitations of dealing with grief. You could trick-or-treat in a different neighborhood, just like you could change jobs, change friends, change houses, change everything to get away from what happened, but it wasn't going to work. Doing something different makes the pain easier to bear but doesn't erase it, almost like you're putting on a different kind of costume to pretend to be someone you're not. The person behind that mask had still suffered the loss of someone who's not coming back. You can't escape the pain or make believe you're really the person you dressed up as instead.

As the weeks and months passed, I felt less prone to talk about last November, and clearly, fewer people wanted to hear about it anymore. They'd moved on. Time had started winding for them again, while for me a part of it remained forever frozen. You end up internalizing things more, coming to grips with the fact that it's just you now. No more casseroles, a house full of people, or people calling to check on you all the time. The phone goes from ringing constantly to practically not at all, and sometimes I still get a cold caller asking for Andy. For a while I'd say, "He's not home right now," or "He's not available." Now, I just hang up.

It was around the six-month mark, in May, when I realized I had to figure out what my next steps were, who I wanted to be, what I was going to do, and how I was going to handle my future. Start moving forward instead of the *Alice in Wonderland* kind of existence where you have to go faster and faster just to stay in the same place. With time, you realize it's all on you. Nobody else is responsible for your grief, and you've got to figure out how to not just get through it, but how to live with it and incorporate it into your life because it is never going anywhere.

Here's a Facebook message I posted right around Halloween, accompanied by a video collage culled from the past year:

> As the week of Andy's passing approaches, I've reflected back on this last year a lot. I often asked people last November, how am I going to do this? And the best advice I got was to let myself feel it and to go right through it. I told myself 2024 would be my yes year. To not say no to the holidays, vacations, reunions, weddings, and gatherings that Andy's absence would be obvious at. And I'm glad I didn't. These memories and people served as a huge part of my healing. Life can still be beautiful after loss and messy at the same time. Grief is so incredibly complicated.
>
> This week represents the last things we did together and the last conversations we had. Trick-or-treating on Court Street in Woodstock, picking out Adalyn's Halloween costume, and

> finalizing our house plans. Our last date, a simple coffee and conversation at Starbucks.
>
> Life changes so quickly. Sometimes I am reminded of my old life and sometimes it's unrecognizable.

Ultimately, it's all on me to figure out what comes next. A year ago, I depended on other people for so much. As time passed, I'd come around to depending on myself, probably more than I ever have in my life. There are still moments where I don't know how I'm going to get through but fewer and fewer of them as time goes by. Facebook posts I've been making like the one above have become more than check-ins; they're debriefs on this journey I've been on, and the vast majority of the pictures that accompany them are of my life after The Call, since both my mind and Facebook pages are already crammed with memories of Andy.

A single moment—that's all it takes for life to change drastically and forever. On Halloween night, trick-or-treating through that neighborhood, I wore no costume because my life was already totally unrecognizable from what it had been a year ago. Everything I felt about life was different. Absolutely nothing was the same and never will be again. Accepting that was the first stage of moving forward for me.

And, toward that end, I've crawled out of the hole I couldn't stop crawling into a year ago.

CHAPTER 16

The Magic Track Suit

Here's a Facebook post I made one year to the day after The Call, the very day the inaugural Andy King Memorial 5K took place:

> The difference of a year. November 2, 2023. 2:54 p.m. "We did everything we could, Mrs. King, but your husband didn't survive." I've spent time the last ten days processing where I was this time last year. I've replayed the abrupt phone call one hundred times over, our last call that morning, our last text fifteen minutes prior, his body's procession home, the funeral, my friends and family coming out to sign the wood studs of the home we were building. Fast forward to November 2, 2024. The week I moved into that new home, the week of the last first holiday without Andy, Halloween. The week of the first annual Andy King Memorial 5K. The

> week that the ending to my book finishes. It has been a hell of a year. I am hopeful. I am sad. I am content. I am scared. I am happy. I feel guilt. I am proud. I feel love. One second. Make no mistake, that's all it takes for life as you know it to change forever. No goodbyes. No last words. No take backs.

I yelled the words "Ready, set, go!" from the PA system. After speaking those words from the bleachers of Massanutten Military Academy back in Woodstock, the grounds on which Andy was buried, I sped down the steps and off I went.

I ran alongside my sister Nicole and best friend Lydia the whole time, among the other 233 registrants. That was especially appropriate, given that our high school cross country and track coach, Nancy Specht, who's now seventy-two, walked the course with me when I was organizing the 5K. I reached out to ask for her assistance and expertise. I hadn't spoken to Nancy in ten years, but it turned out she was on the other side of Route 81 the day of Andy's procession. She saw all the people and displays on the overpasses and didn't realize it was for Andy, whom she had also coached, until later. I reached out to her when I started the planning process, not realizing it was the first step in reconnecting with our collective past.

To commemorate that, my sister and I paid a small fortune to purchase these old-school matching track suits on eBay in navy because I wanted the 5K to have a red, white, and blue theme. They were actually called "Vintage Track Suits," matching the ones we'd worn in high school when Andy was there to watch my cross country meets. Maybe that track suit I wore would turn out to be magical. Maybe donning it would wind back time and give me a chance to relive the years when my dad was still alive, Andy was still alive, and I was just a soft, innocent high school kid before I'd been hardened by death. There is you before death and you after death. And I often long for the before, when I was still carefree and untouched by life's harshest realities.

The nostalgia that dominated the day evolved into a communal experience populated by different people from different stages of my life dating all the way back to childhood. Andy's funeral, I suppose, had been that as well, but the 5K felt so much different because we were celebrating instead of mourning him. It seemed like the perfect way to honor Andy not only because all the proceeds, around $25,000 that included generous sponsorships, would go to his Memorial Scholarship Fund, but also because he had been a runner himself.

It was still dark, chilly, and cold when I arrived. Alone, the only one on the grounds of Massanutten Military Academy, and I was back in Woodstock. That moment made me eerily feel that although a year had passed, nothing had changed. Worse, this was the time Andy would have been putting on his uniform, loading up his gear, and tucking it into the back of that Humvee one year ago today. As I drove by myself at five a.m. to the race in the dark, that was all I could think of.

Then the sun peeked out and volunteers started to arrive, including the local bakery that was donating the pastries, coffee, and juice. And by the time the cars started piling into the parking lot, their headlights slicing through the last of the predawn dark, that eerie feeling dissipated and then vanished altogether as the sun rose into a crystal-clear blue sky.

A college friend of mine named Tucker Wyatt, who lived in the area, was among that first phalanx to arrive. He had texted me weeks before when he heard about the 5K:

HEY, WOULD YOU LIKE FREE MUSIC?

Tucker was in a band, but he went solo that day, bringing not only the country music songs he'd made his own but also the PA system I used to say a prayer over everyone, marking the first time I'd ever prayed over a group of people, which was a big deal for me. All the runners and spectators were crowded onto the track below, spilling out onto the football field.

"Thanks to you," I said in part, "Andy King is still here. I want this run to be about us, remembering the qualities of Andy we loved and living them in our everyday lives."

I had two banners made for the occasion. One of them read ANDY KING MEMORIAL 5K and had all the sponsorship logos on it. The second featured a giant photo of me, Andy, and Adalyn. As soon as Addie saw it when she arrived, she said, "I wanna sit with my dada." I realized in that moment that's why I had done all of this, that it was all for her. All these events the last year served as a chance for Addie to remember her dada with everyone. And Addie saying that one little line made everything worth it.

I also asked two of my friends if they could bring the same giant American flag they had hung over one of the overpasses the day of Andy's procession a year ago. They brought in these twin towering pieces of equipment to string the giant flag across the front of the track. I knew how pumped Andy would be to have it out there and could hear his voice in my head saying, "Hell yeah!" with his sideways grin.

I had walked or driven the course more times than I could count, but it felt different running the actual race. We passed a house Andy and I had toured but opted not to buy, after which the course strung onto the same route we'd taken that final Halloween night, covering half the route. With all the hills, the course itself was like a roller coaster, a fitting metaphor for the past year. The hills of grief that got steeper and steeper, before finally leveling off, only to dip and rise again. The farther I ran, the more the hills lightened and the downhill stretches increased. Near the end, after the steepest hill of them all, the course flattened out entirely and I coasted the final stretch to the finish line. And, appropriately enough, we all followed spray-painted arrows with "AKK" for Anderson Keaton King, directing runners along the course, as if Andy was pointing them in the right direction.

Tucker played throughout the morning as people mixed and mingled, some stretching and filling up the water bottles they would then strap to their sides. The air and energy felt very calm and peaceful. It was exactly how I wanted the day to be.

Included among them was Sean from Helena, Andy's good friend and coworker who had spoken at his funeral. I don't think many of the people who came were huge 5K runners, but just like them, Sean insisted on running this one. I could also feel Andy cracking up that Sean was doing this for him, because they were polar opposites when it came to running and training. And, I know Andy was cheering loudly for him as he neared the finish line.

Andy's commanding officer, Lieutenant Colonel Aaron Hall, ran the race too. I'd rarely seen him smile before. I felt like I was looking at a different person than the one I'd met last year. We were all different, we had all been changed by this, from someone who had known Andy for five minutes to five years. Everybody there had a smile on their face. Nobody cried. Just the way it should have been, the way Andy would have wanted it, a celebration of hope. So many of the people there had built this legacy with me, and all of us were transformed from who we'd been a year ago, whether we realized it or not.

That included the Army bereavement officer, Scott, who showed up at my door the day after The Call and eventually brought Andy's duffel bags home to me that I'd watched Andy pack five days earlier. On this morning, he showed up in running gear with a smile on his face, flowers in hand for me, and his beautiful family by his side. No longer viewed by me as the person who delivered sadness but as someone I now considered a friend. We had spent the last year together, through his delivering tough news and having difficult conversations every week in the beginning. From me crying at my kitchen table every time he arrived to our relationship morphing into `How are you?? texts and How can I help with the 5K? and I can't wait to see you and your family and friends again.` He never even met Andy, but I believe he emerged a different person from the experience anyway.

As I crossed the finish line with my sister Nicole by my side, the past year came to both a figurative and literal close. I felt light, refreshed, fulfilled, even jubilant. Over that final stretch I couldn't help but think, *Amy, you did everything you said you were gonna do this year, I am so damn proud of you.* I honored Andy and integrated his legacy into my life with memories our daughter will hold on to for as long as her toddler mind allows. After that, the pictures and the flags and the stories will keep her dad forever at the forefront of her mind. I buried Andy, created the scholarship fund in his name, organized the 5K, and, yes, wrote this book. I felt so much pride, spent in the company of so many of the people who had helped get me there. I could not have integrated joy and grief into my life so well without the help of all of them. That said, I felt in that moment I was finally standing on my own two feet.

It's been a year now. And that feels crazy to say out loud. A year that has reshaped everything I thought I knew about life and about myself. Grief doesn't politely knock and wait for you to be ready. It tears through your world, unmaking it, piece by piece. And even though the days keep passing, even though the seasons change and the sun still rises, nothing looks the same. How could it? How could I expect life to return to the way it was, when the person I was back then is gone too?

There was a time when I thought I'd circle back, that eventually, after enough time, I'd find my way back to the version of life that existed before loss entered the room. But grief taught me otherwise. There is no returning. There is only moving forward, reshaped, scarred, altered but still moving. I've had to accept that some doors have closed forever, that some chapters don't get rewritten. And in that acceptance, slowly, quietly, a different life begins to unfold.

It doesn't mean I've left the loss behind. It's stitched into me now, part of the fabric of who I am. But I've realized that staying frozen in the shadow of grief isn't living, it's surviving. And I want more than survival. I owe it to myself, and to the love I carry for what I've lost, to keep going. It's not the life I planned, but it's the life I have, and even amidst the sorrow, there's space for hope, for rebuilding, for moments of joy that surprise me when I least expect them.

I was the last to leave the grounds of Massanutten Military Academy, just as I'd been the first to arrive, and felt as if I was leaving a piece of me behind there, the piece that would allow me to move forward now. I felt so much pressure to be strong over the last year and to create a legacy for Andy that could be carried forward every year for Addie and me. As I drove off the grounds, though, I didn't feel that pressure anymore. This day had been an opportunity to show everyone that even in the depths of darkness, there is hope. The grief will stay with us all as we leave, but this time with more hope and joy than a year ago. This year was very hard on many people, not just me. Andy's family, my friends, his coworkers, his beloved farmers. We are all survivors.

A bunch of us gathered at the Woodstock Brewhouse afterward. The town was awash in a sea of people wearing the souvenir 5K T-shirts that still had their bib numbers in place. People waved and yelled out to me as I drove from one end of Woodstock to the other. Just as all those flowers from Andy's funeral had spread him out along Main Street a year before, he was spread out everywhere again, his memory and his legacy stronger than ever.

And this time, there was something else. All the spray paint on the roads with "AKK" arrows remained in place for weeks, pointing forward, down a route that led into the future. With the race now over, it was almost like Andy was still showing everyone the way. That's what I want his legacy to feel like, living out the qualities about him we so loved and cherished, forever.

The picture of Addie spending some time under the banner with her dada, the giant American flag strung in the background, is so frozen in memory I'll never have to look at it again. But I probably will.

Because the banner is dominated by a portrait of the three of us together. Forever.

Andy's family and I gathered at Andy's grave before leaving the grounds. Everyone who'd completed the 5K was awarded a Finisher's Medal as they crossed the finish line, and we laid one on Andy's gravestone, which was so appropriate because we all knew he had run the race with us. I went back a week or so after, and the medal was gone. Maybe the wind had whisked it away. Maybe a storm had buried it in the ground. Or maybe Andy's wearing it up in the sky, having finished a winner.

Forever, too.

EPILOGUE

When Grief and Joy Coexist

On Saturday afternoon just before Thanksgiving in 2024, I was in Carolina Beach, North Carolina, falling in and out of sleep. Not a momentous occasion for most, I know, but it marked the first time in over a year that I could nap in peace without my mind racing. I can hear Addie giggling and playing in the next room. She is happy. She is loved. And she has seen her mom happy and loved as well.

In September, I downloaded a dating app called Hinge as a kind of joke with my best friend Lydia. I wasn't really serious about meeting someone that way. It was more lighthearted and a way to start putting myself out there because it was something I knew I was ready for. I had spent the last ten months immersed in my grief and coming to terms with my new reality. I never shied away from that and used that time to accept, heal, and process in large part through writing this book. I knew I was in a place where I was ready to add someone to my life. I was ready to be Amy again, the new Amy I had to become. I was ready to meet someone who could get to know *this* Amy. I was ready to be just myself with someone. Not mom, not daughter, not sister, not friend, not widow. I set my profile to Fort Mill, where Adam and Caylee lived in South Carolina, because I didn't want to meet anyone in my area.

Little did I know I was getting closer to the person I was becoming.

Lydia and I would go through our potential matches on FaceTime and sometimes reply to people who jumped out at us for one reason or another. I didn't think I was really serious about this, until it turned out I was.

One of the potential matches that came up on my feed was named Tim, who, if he was telling the truth about his age, was thirty-one to my twenty-eight. His profile grabbed my attention because it featured a question as a kind of game:

HERE ARE TWO TRUTHS AND A LIE. WHICH ONE IS THE LIE?

I responded, and deleted the app almost immediately because it was all just for fun. I wasn't going to date anyone from Hinge, right? Now that I'd yanked the app off my phone, I'd never know if Tim replied, nor did I think twice about it.

A few weeks later, I was at a rehearsal dinner in Maryland on a Thursday night with the wedding of a good friend set to take place the following day. Everyone at the dinner except me was with their significant others, which left me feeling a bit lonely and left out. So, out of boredom while I was sitting alone, I downloaded the Hinge app again to see if I could find someone to chat with. As soon as I logged on to my revived profile, I saw that Tim had responded to the original post I had left for him weeks before:

YOU'RE RIGHT! HA-HA!

He was talking about those two truths and a lie that I'd correctly identified. Tim sent a second message shortly after the first, but I never saw that one either because I'd deleted the app. I reached back out to him, and we actually started talking that night and hit it off immediately. We talked about Andy, we talked about his divorce. The evening of the wedding, all I could think about was how much I was looking forward to speaking to him again, and that night we spoke until around two o'clock in the morning and then scheduled a FaceTime date for Monday night when I'd be back home. The date lasted over two hours, and we proceeded to FaceTime every day for the next two weeks.

When I went down to South Carolina in the beginning of October to visit Adam and Caylee, we had our first in-person date, Tim got to meet Adalyn, and I felt this deep connection on an emotional level. Tim checked all the boxes I never thought I'd ever see checked again. I might not have seen this relationship coming, but I loved the view. Tim knew only the bare facts gleaned from my profile before we met, but he quickly came to embrace all the details about Addie, me, and Andy too.

Both he and Andy were dedicated, hardworking individuals who cared about faith, family, and their health above everything else. Here I was, dating a person I'd met on an app who happened to be everything I wanted for Addie and me. I tell Tim all the time that I can picture Andy saying to God, "Send Amy your best. She doesn't need to suffer in the dating world for long. She's been through enough." Tim was a deeply emotional and secure person. Someone who gave me space to grieve and love in my own ways, and someone who was clearly capable of handling my glass heart, as well as Addie's.

A month or so into our fledgling relationship, Addie joined a FaceTime call with Tim and me. I'd been worried for a while about her forgetting Andy, because we'd been talking to Tim more, and with all the moving I hadn't hung any of the pictures Addie used to kiss before bed. I'd been feeling guilty about that, and I finally pulled some out of the boxes to hang in our new house the night before that call. And she picked up exactly where she left off, kissing and hugging Andy before she went to bed.

She'd gotten a lot more verbal as of late, so on the FaceTime call I asked her about her day in school. She started talking about her little friend in class Roland, which was nice because I'm good friends with Roland's parents.

"Roland's dada picked him up today," she told me, followed by, "I miss my daddy."

"I miss your daddy too, and it's okay to miss him," I managed, choking back tears.

"But I love you, Mommy."

"Would you like to see a photo of your dad?" I asked her, through the lump that had formed in my throat.

Addie nodded again. "Yes."

So I went and got her favorite picture.

"I want to show Tim. I miss my daddy, I love my mommy, and I want to show Tim my daddy."

And with that she held the picture up before my phone on our FaceTime call.

Tim's jaw hit the floor. He'd built his life around his Christian faith. He'd been praying for signs that he was doing the right thing by Addie and me. Now, Addie had acknowledged me, him, and Andy all within sixty seconds.

I do believe faith is the reason Addie and I have made it as far as we have. I've learned to trust in the fact there is a greater plan and believe all this has been part of that plan. Someday, we will all understand why everything happens the way it does, but until then I will trust in God's plan, and that continues to be what keeps me going.

Not long after that call, I met Tim's family for the first time. He was very open about the fact that his dad was a recovering alcoholic but had been sober for thirty-one years since learning Tim was going to be born. During that trip to Fort Mill, his parents asked me about my parents, and I told them about my father's struggles.

I watched Tim's dad stiffen. "Did Tim tell you about me?"

"Yes, and I'm very proud of you being sober for so long." There are many parts about Tim, and his family, that helped nurture my healing. Talking to his dad was like getting a peak at what could have been for my dad.

That conversation made Tim's mom and dad feel like family to me. It was just the three of us sitting at their dining room table after my first dinner in their home. I wasn't used to having in-laws, and they were not used to having a daughter-in-law who wanted a relationship with them.

I had been feeling a bit suffocated in Woodstock, the little town that had provided so much comfort and served as my support system through the worst months imaginable in the wake of receiving The Call. I love my friends, my church, and the community and don't know where I'd be without them, but I believe I've outgrown the Woodstock I loved so much. And it's no one's fault. After something like this happens, you will never be the same again. Whoever I was before The Call died on November 2, 2023, right alongside Andy, and I had to fully embrace that before growing beyond it. I love and appreciate everything Woodstock gave me, but it became so hard to be there. It felt more like a place I want to visit and hold in my memory, the place Andy and I started our family, and the place I said goodbye to him. It felt like a place I needed to keep sacred to us, and there was no us without him. When I am outside of Woodstock, I am just Amy. I can be my own person again, not an older version of myself forever identified by loss. It felt wrong to continue life there with someone new.

I know in my heart that something brought Andy and me to Woodstock, and that was more than borne out by those initial months after The Call. Two things, though, can be true at once. This was the place that saved me, and it became the place where I felt like a hostage to myself. A place that helped me hold my ground became an anchor holding me back. I lost my husband, and everyone else in Woodstock lost a friend. The thing is, they don't have to move forward like I do. They don't need someone to fill the role Andy played in their lives like I do. I have a husband role to fill and a father role to fill. My entire identity and family dynamic were turned upside down. Andy and I would probably be having our second kid right now, living in our dream house. My life is so far removed from what it was and what it will be. I am envious of those who get to go home at night to their same evening routine with every member of their family in it, because my family will never be fully complete again. I'll never manage to find that sense of comfort for me and Addie, unless I move forward, and even then, it will never be the same.

I only had one husband. I've got no backup here, and so I have to try and fill that role.

When Tim came to visit Addie and me for the first time, I felt hesitant to bring him around town. I was concerned it might be difficult for others to understand, much less accept, our relationship, and I wanted to protect him from any discomfort that might arise from being seen as someone stepping into Andy

King's place. I'm slowly finding my way toward acceptance, processing everything as it comes and reflecting deeply along the way.

When I introduced Tim to people, I could sense that it was hard for them. Some hadn't really seen me since the funeral, and that meant this was their first real moment of confronting the loss. I've come to see that some people needed more time. They may not have begun grieving Andy yet. For me, for Addie, and for our families, the loss was immediate and constant. We couldn't turn away from it, not for a moment. But for others it may have felt more distant. That's not their fault and I don't blame that at all.

I've learned that everyone has their own path through grief. And while I can't always walk that path with them, I understand that their process is just as real and valid. I've had to face Andy's absence every day, and accepting that has been essential for my healing and for making space to move forward.

I've come to understand that love after loss doesn't erase the love that came before. My love for Andy will always live in me. It shaped who I am and gave me Addie. That kind of love doesn't disappear; it becomes part of your foundation. And yet I also believe we are capable of loving again, in new and different ways, without it being a betrayal of the past.

Tim isn't replacing Andy; no one ever could do that. He's in addition to, not instead of. What he brings into my life is something entirely his own. It's not about comparison but about opening my heart again, carefully and honestly. I know that can be hard for some people to understand, especially those who are still holding on tightly to Andy's memory. I honor that.

At the same time, I've had to give myself permission to keep living, to find joy where I can, and to build something new—not because I've forgotten, but because I remember so deeply. I'm grateful for the love I've had and the love I have now, and I carry both with me every day.

My family and Andy's brothers and their wives are immensely supportive of Tim and me, which has been a beautiful thing to witness.

"We looked at you, and we didn't think we were going to get our sister back," my brother Vinnie said about those initial awful months. "We were concerned that you would never be okay again and we didn't know what to do, because we couldn't fix it. Now, we're so happy to see you smile like this—like, we haven't seen you do that in so long."

I attended a wedding for one of my good friends, Lindsey, in June of 2023 prior to meeting Tim. Her mom passed when she was a teen, so she knows what it's like to be missing somebody. What stood out about Lindsey's wedding was that it was the first time I'd heard the words "'til death do us part" spoken as part of a couple's vows since Andy had passed. All I could think of was, *Oh wow, I actually lived that.* I don't think many people, when they get married, realize what they're saying. How could they, though? How could they understand the gravity of those words until it happens? Even still, during the vows and thinking back to when Andy and I said ours, I felt so happy. Sadness did not overtake me, I still love *love*, and I still hope to share vows with someone again one day. I feel that so deeply and it resonates so strongly.

The thing about Tim and me is that we're both healing and both ready to continue that process with someone. He's experienced his own pain with his divorce. We both know what we want, and neither of us is about to settle for anything less. We both have extremely high standards. I think about how I felt during Andy's last Halloween looking at all those glow sticks lighting the world ahead, what awaited me down that bright tunnel. This Halloween, I could only see the light from the glow sticks that were right before me, and that's the way I manage life now. I'm not going to extensively plan a future in full knowledge of how quickly things can change. God doesn't care what your plan is. It's better, I've learned, to live in the moment. I don't even look at the weather for tomorrow anymore because I am too focused on today. If something or someone makes me happy, I'm going to go with it.

It's difficult to hear things like, "We're not judging you, but..." because even the gentlest disclaimers can still carry a weight of misunderstanding. I know it often comes from a place of care or confusion, but unless someone has experienced a loss that shakes the very ground beneath them, it's hard to truly grasp the path I've walked. There is no right way or wrong way to grieve a loss this devastating; there is only your way. No one analyzes my decisions more than I, and only I have to live with the ones that I make.

For over a year, I've sat with my grief fully, consciously, and without running from it. I didn't numb myself or shut it out. I faced it every single night, often alone, and I sought help through my support systems and honest reflection. That journey wasn't easy, but it brought me to where I am now, a place of hard-earned readiness and acceptance of life as it is now.

I understand that from the outside, it might be easier to question or make assumptions, especially if your world remains largely intact. But I've had to rebuild from the inside out. And while I know I will never be fully healed, because grief isn't something that simply disappears, I'm committed to showing up for my life, and for my daughter, every single day and integrating this grief into it.

Six years ago, I thought losing my dad was the greatest pain I would ever endure. Until I lost Andy. Now, I live with the awareness that nothing is promised, and because of that I choose to embrace joy, to welcome love, and to seek out light wherever I can find it. Not because I've moved on, but because I'm still moving, carried by love, by hope, and by gratitude.

Tim's trip to Woodstock became a kind of revelation for me, as I watched the dynamic unfold of him developing a relationship with Adalyn. I say that because cooking and having dinner together, then following Addie's usual bedtime routine, felt like my old life of normalcy before The Call.

Addie, meanwhile, has been laughing the hardest I've ever seen her laugh. She's giggling all the time, either feeding off the change in my mood or finding comfort in having Tim in her life.

That first day she met Tim, we went to a park. There was a pumpkin-decorating contest going on, and one of the pumpkins on display featured a patriot theme, dominated by an American flag. As we passed it, Addie pointed and said to Tim, "That's my dada's flag."

I found myself overwhelmed by her grasp of the situation, that two things could indeed be true at once, since she could have Tim in her life while still acknowledging Andy as her father.

Around that same time, I took Addie to his grave for the first time since the burial so we could leave flowers. I explained what we were doing here to her, and she nodded.

"Dada can see me, but he's hiding from me."

That was the first time she said anything like that, anything beyond *Dada's in the sky*. But now she says stuff to that effect all the time, like "He's hiding from us." And now she says, "Grandpa's hiding too."

That new perspective, I think, came courtesy of us starting to play hide-and-seek at home after Addie learned it at day care, and she's articulating more and more about her feelings, relating the game to the father she lost and grandfather she never knew.

"Daddy's hiding and he can see me, but I can't see him" was how she put it next, and she says that all the time now.

Tim and I began FaceTiming while I was still living at my mother's house, and it was hard because I kept looking for more signs, something definitive, of Andy showing me *This is what you need.* One afternoon, when we were FaceTiming, Adalyn was playing around in the closet and shut the door on herself with Tim watching.

"Where'd Addie go?" he said.

Addie opened the door and said, "Boo!"

I got chills up and down my spine, because a few weeks before Andy died I remembered him hiding behind the little play couch in Addie's room with her sitting on one of the cushions pretending she didn't know where he was, until she heard his voice.

"*Where'd Addie go?*"

AFTERWORD

Two Things Can Be True at the Same Time

In February of 2025, Adalyn met Mickey Mouse for the first time at Disney World. But that was just the finale in a whirlwind of events that have set my life down a new path. This part of my journey was stoked by the fact I realized I can miss Andy and still fall in love again, mourn him and still be happy.

Two things really can be true at the same time.

As it turned out, my dream home on the property Andy and I bought together proved to be anything but that. I wanted more than anything to love and embrace it, but I never did. So much so that after a few weeks there, Addie and I moved back in with my mom. Woodstock had been everything we wanted and needed when we first settled there. We met and bonded with our friends and church and genuinely believed we had found our place in the world.

We...

I realized that the life Andy and I had built around the Woodstock community needed to remain as that, and I needed to find my own world with just me in it. I genuinely believe fate called me to Woodstock, just as I believe it was only supposed to be a stepping stone in my life instead of a final destination. I will always cherish everything the town meant to me, even while acknowledging the realization it had become impossible for me to live there anymore. I can love my friends there, and remain profoundly grateful for their support during the most difficult time of my life, and still move forward from the world in which Andy and I would be raising our kids together and living in Woodstock forever.

Because two things can be true at the same time.

I felt like I was stuck, that if I stayed in this world that I no longer embraced I would never be able to find myself and who I was moving forward. It was never going to feel right starting over with someone else there.

My mom and sister both asked me why I was staying.

"I don't know why you're still here," my mom kept saying.

It wasn't that easy to leave, especially since I was afraid I was doing too much, one thing after another. I often wondered what my grief process would be like had I never left my Woodstock house and stayed in our family home where I said goodbye to Andy. Then Adam said something that really resonated with me.

"Amy, we can go back to the past and live in it, but Andy's not going to be there."

I had never thought about it that way, that you can't let death define you and determine your every decision. Until that moment, I think I'd been afraid to move forward and know I'm far from alone in the exclusive community of young widows I'm a part of, a club nobody wants to join. The truth of the matter is, moving to another state or falling in love with someone new has no bearing on your grief. Your grief is still there and will be forever. If anything, it actually makes you confront it more. You will always miss the person you lost multiple times every day and think about them every morning. Those parts never go away whether you stay where you are or move forward.

In December of 2024, I started looking for houses in the Fort Mill, South Carolina, area and almost immediately settled on this five-bedroom colonial. It was so perfect, compared to what had come to feel more like a garage apartment where I was sleeping on a pull-down bed, that I made an offer sight unseen. Building that house just outside of Woodstock had been the right thing to do at the time, just like buying this one in Fort Mill was. Twenty-four hours later, the house was under contract, and I felt instantly liberated, like I was going where life wanted to take me.

I'd practically be neighbors with Adam, Caylee, and my twin nephews. Of course, there was also Tim and his family living mere minutes away. Embracing the new instead of holding fast to the old.

I closed on the house, but before we moved in, we made that trip to Disney World—me and my two Disney kids, Tim and Addie. His family had gone to Disney almost every other year pretty much all his life, so he knew all the ins and outs of the park. It was an amazing experience, but not for the reasons I had expected. When we left for the trip, Addie was into Winnie the Pooh, Mickey Mouse, and the Disney cast of regulars. Our first day at the park, the line to meet Mickey was only ten minutes long. She greeted him with a hug, and I don't think there was a dry eye in the room. When she met Pluto, Addie told him all about our dogs. Listening to her, I was amazed at how much more verbal she had become over the last few months, stringing sentences together and becoming quite the conversationalist. Her favorite attraction was the Ariel ride, and she couldn't wait to meet Ariel's character as well.

After that, Ariel was all she could talk about, and I realized she had graduated from Mickey and Pluto to her princess era. An Ariel doll purchased by her Auntie Nicole on the last night was her favorite souvenir from the trip, and I couldn't help tearing up over the thought she wasn't a baby anymore. Watching her and Tim together on the trip served to convince me even more of his devotion to Addie and desire to be a great father figure to her. And I could see how much having a male figure in her life again meant to her. The truth is kids at this age are really trying to figure out their familial units. Addie is constantly asking me who is the dad and who is the mom in some of her friends' families. There was a moment at a children's farm where she was looking at the horses.

"I love the horses, Mommy," she said.

"Oh, your daddy would have loved to hear you say that. He loved horses too," I responded, still always trying to teach her more about Andy.

She looked at me and said, "What is my daddy's name?"

I smiled. "Andy."

"Yeah, and my other daddy's name is Tim."

I had no idea how to respond. Moments like these are so hard for me. I love that she feels so safe with Tim, and at the same time my heart shatters into a million pieces that Andy doesn't get to hear his baby girl call him "daddy." She doesn't actually call Tim that, but she is definitely starting to see him as that type of figure in her life.

I see so much judgment from other young widows online whose kids call someone else daddy now. And the truth is, this isn't something we force on our kids. This is something that our kids find comfort in. It is something they crave. And if referring to Tim as that makes Addie feel comfortable and safe, then I am not going to correct her. I will admit that I was adamant about Andy being the only one ever known as "dad" to her because he was, and it was a role he took so seriously. But this is about her journey and her feelings, not mine. She recognizes a paternal love with Tim that she hasn't felt since Andy, and she is placing that in her brain by referring to Tim as her dad. And I won't be the one to confuse her even more, after all she has endured by my side.

We moved into our new house shortly after returning from Orlando, and one of the first things we did was hang up the same pictures that had hung in the hall of our house in Woodstock, except this time we added one of Tim and Addie. I'd never put them up in the Edinburg house, because it never felt like home. That enabled Addie to resume her practice of kissing Andy's picture before she went to bed at night, and I was awestruck by the fact of how well she recalled performing that ritual back in Woodstock. We don't really know what toddlers are capable of, and Addie always manages to surprise me.

The first night after I hung the pictures, she couldn't wait to show Tim.

"Look, Tim," she said, pointing to her favorite, "it's me and Dada."

She sounded so proud, almost like she was introducing him to Andy. And she remains adamant that it's the four of us together, not three, when she says who her family members are. Tim actually helped me get her potty-trained, his first major milestone as a father figure, and he was beaming so much his face was glowing.

Meanwhile, Addie loves the new house.

She also loves living in Fort Mill, period. She's the happiest and calmest I've ever seen her. Addie's sleeping through the night and can't wait to show her room to everyone who comes over. That room overlooks our fenced-in backyard packed with mature shade trees, and it's so quiet because we live on a cul-de-sac. We're ten minutes from where Tim lives and the same from Adam and Caylee. Addie will be starting preschool in the same year as twins Charlie and Henry. It feels like a real family again to the point where Adam and I wonder out loud whether we're creating the childhood we wanted to have growing up.

I'm in a good place, and it was a great time to move and embark on a new beginning with a running start. It's fun to be making new friends, settling in with a new church, and getting accustomed to a lifestyle with more stores, shops, and traffic. I'm still going to return to Woodstock for Andy's 5K and many times in between. I will continue to do everything I've planned to honor Andy and continue his legacy, which includes my home drenched in photos of him and, of course, flags. I plan on keeping the house in Edinburg and opening it up as an Airbnb. My family and many friends still live in Virginia, so it's a place I plan to visit often, and I think I will enjoy it more as a tourist than as a resident. Besides Addie, that house is the last thing I have that Andy was a part of, so maybe I'm a bit sentimental about keeping it, while making a new life for myself in Fort Mill.

Because two things can be true at the same time.

We moved into our new house on the Friday before Valentine's Day, and a week later I hosted a Valentine's Day dinner. Tim took Adalyn with him when he went to pick up the food, the two of them watching the sunset on the way home.

"Look," she said, pointing out the window, "my dada sent me a sunset tonight."

And every time Tim would turn the car, Addie saw it from a different angle.

"Oh," she noted happily, "he sent me a lot of sunsets."

She couldn't wait to tell me about it when she got home.

"My dada's in the sky. He made me a sunset." Then she paused. "And Grandpa too!"

"Anyone else?" I asked her.

"No," Addie answered nonchalantly, "I think that's everyone."

ABOUT THE AUTHOR

Amy King was raised in Clarke County, Virginia. She attended Virginia Tech with her high school sweetheart, Andy King, where they studied and pursued careers in Agribusiness Management. In honor of her late husband, Amy created the Andy King Memorial Scholarship, which sponsors an annual 5K fundraising event that supports students pursuing agriculture studies in Virginia. Amy is currently raising her daughter in Fort Mill, South Carolina, and is living for her husband's legacy.